westermann

W0252462

On Track

Workbook

Englisch für Gymnasien

4

von:
Annie Altamirano
Claire Hart
Jon Hird
Patricia Wedler

herausgegeben von:
Helga Holtkamp

Lehrwerk und weitere Begleitmaterialien:

Schulbuch ISBN 978-3-14-040324-5
Medienpaket ISBN 978-3-14-062682-8
Ferienlektüre ISBN 978-3-14-040884-4
Klassenarbeitstrainer ISBN 978-3-7426-0334-0

BiBox – Digitale Unterrichtsmaterialien
Nähere Informationen unter www.bibox.schule

Vokabel-Apps sind online erhältlich.

westermann GRUPPE

Druck A[1] / Jahr 2021
Alle Drucke der Serie A sind inhaltlich unverändert.

Unter Mitarbeit von: Christine House, Sîan Jones

Illustrationen: Karen Donnelly
Umschlaggestaltung: Detlef Möller, Paderborn
Umschlagbild vorne: Downtown skyline over highways at twilight in Chicago, Illinois, USA;
© Sean Pavone / Alamy Stock Photo
Umschlagbild hinten: Kayaks on West Curme Island, British Columbia, Canada;
© All Canada Photos / Alamy Stock Photo
Druck und Bindung: Westermann Druck GmbH, Georg-Westermann-Allee 66, 38104 Braunschweig

ISBN 978-3-14-**040344**-3

How to work with the Workbook

On Track 4 Workbook has a short *Welcome* section and four regular workshops – like your students' book. Every page in your Workbook belongs to a page in your students' book. There is a reference at the top of the page (→ students' book, page 12 etc.). The colours of the pages are also the same. The activities and exercises have numbers, letters and symbols as in your students' book.

The Workbook uses the same symbols as your students' book. You will also find webcodes.

How to use the webcodes

A webcode is like a small website. All the *On Track* audio material that you need for class or homework is here: www.westermann.de/webcodes. You can also find transcripts of the audios and videos. You can listen online or download a folder with everything in it. Type in the code for the workshop (**WES-40344-001**) without the @ and click "Aufrufen" to get to the page for Workshop 1. You know the webcodes from your students' book.

These are the webcodes in *On Track 4 Workbook*:

Welcome: @ WES-40344-000
Workshop 1: @ WES-40344-001
Workshop 2: @ WES-40344-002
Workshop 3: @ WES-40344-003
Workshop 4: @ WES-40344-004

Der **Grammatikanhang** erklärt alle Grammatikregeln, die du in *On Track 4* lernst. Dein *Workbook* enthält den gleichen Anhang wie dein Schulbuch. Du kannst die Grammatikseiten aus dem *Workbook* z. B. in einer Mappe sammeln und hast so immer alle wichtigen Regeln parat.

Contents

→ students' book, pages 10/11

What do you know about the USA?

1 Famous places in the USA

a Look up the places below on the internet. Then look at the map of the USA and put the place names in the correct box.

New York ■ Disney World ■ The Grand Canyon ■ Los Angeles ■ Mount Rushmore ■ Chicago

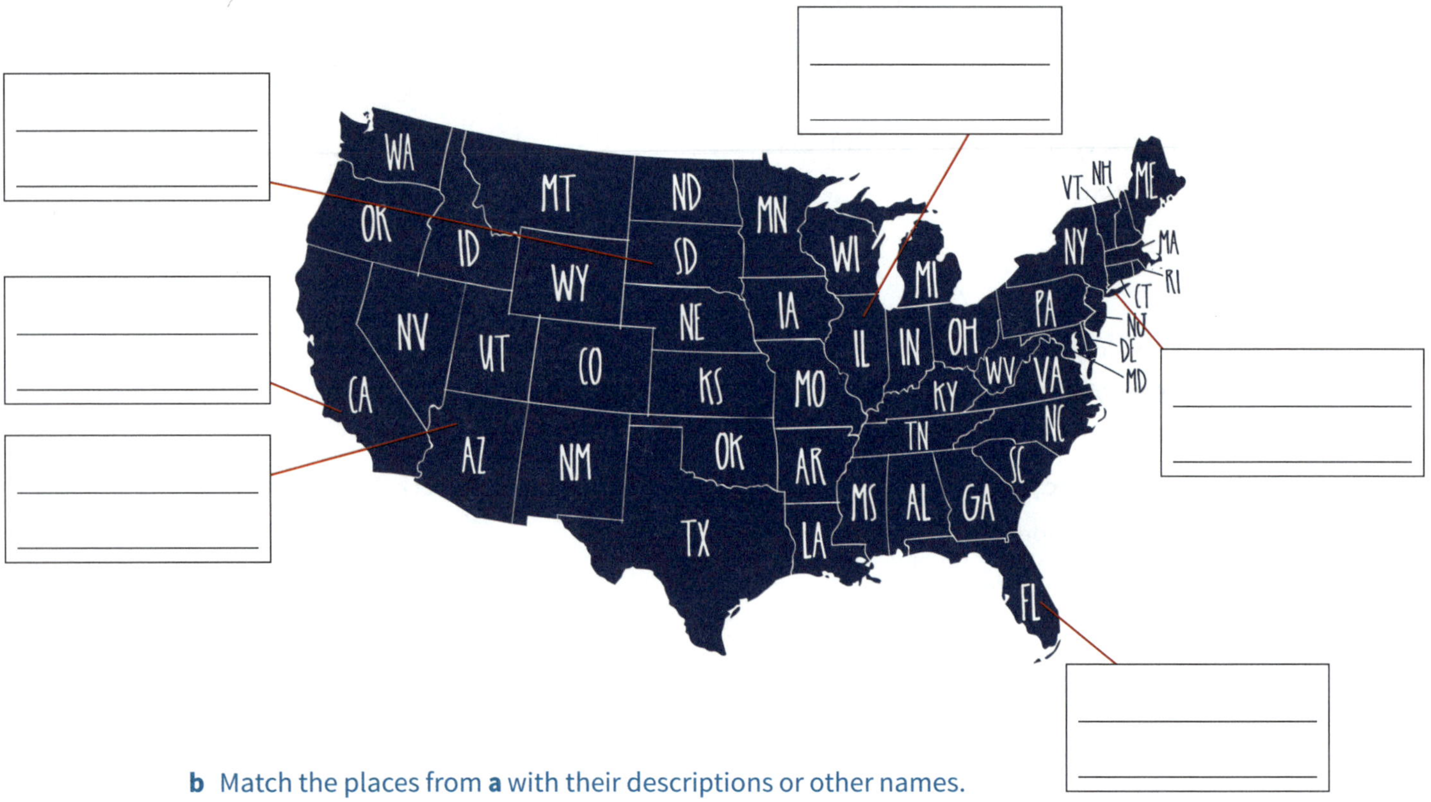

b Match the places from **a** with their descriptions or other names.

The Big Apple	a popular theme park in Florida
Disney World	Chicago
The Grand Canyon	a stone monument to presidents of the USA
Los Angeles	the film capital of the world
Mount Rushmore	New York
The Windy City	a national park in Arizona

c Get together with a partner. Tell him / her which of these places you would most like to visit and explain why.

2 Famous Americans

a Listen to an American history teacher telling her class about three famous Americans: Steve Jobs, Alexander Hamilton and Harriet Tubman. Number the people in the order they were born. Then match the names to the pictures.

☐ Steve Jobs ☐ Alexander Hamilton ☐ Harriet Tubman

A

____

B

____

C

____

b Listen again and answer the questions in complete sentences.

1 Which country did Steve Jobs' father come from?

____.

2 How old was Steve Jobs when he was fired from Apple?

____.

3 Which company did Jobs found after he was fired?

____.

4 Which city did Harriet Tubman go to after she escaped from slavery?

____.

5 How many slaves did Harriet Tubman help to escape?

____.

6 What did Harriet Tubman do during the American Civil War?

____.

7 Where was Alexander Hamilton born?

____.

8 Which famous group of men was Alexander Hamilton a member of?

____.

c Work in a group. Think of a question you would like to ask each of these three famous Americans. Say the answer that you think each person would give.

Ms Tubman, were your ever scared when you were helping slaves to escape?
Yes, of course, but …

Living in the USA

1 A different place

a Read the comments on Ellie Quinn's blogpost and her replies. Answer the questions.

1 Who wants Ellie to give some advice? ______________________

2 Who is interested in differences in the language? ______________________

3 Who wants to know how Ellie feels about something she has to do in the USA? ______________________

4 Who starts their comment with something positive and then criticizes Ellie? ______________________

5 Who doesn't think that Ellie's life in the USA is as good as it seems? ______________________

6 Who reads Ellie's blog while they're travelling? ______________________

1 Hi Ellie! Learning about your experiences in the USA is extremely interesting. You mention that some words are different in British English and American English, like 'pavement' and 'sidewalk'. I was wondering if it's difficult to remember to use the *correct* American English and if you sometimes get confused between the two types of English. – **Natalya**

Hi Natalya! Thanks for your comment. Getting used to new words for everyday things isn't always easy. But when you hear them all the time, it helps you to remember. It's a bit like learning a foreign language – remembering the words, then using them when you speak!

2 Thank you for your posts, Ellie! Reading them on the bus to school makes time go by a lot faster! I've started planning my year abroad in the USA next year. Would you recommend staying with a host family or is it better to live on your own? – **Sam**

Hi Sam! Thank you for your comment. I thought about living on my own when I started to plan my year, too, but now I'm glad I'm with a host family. I like being part of a family and helping out with all the chores. They can give you a lot of practical tips when you first arrive and introduce you to people. My recommendation would be to stay with a host family.

3 Hey Ellie! I find your blog very interesting. However, I can't help asking myself if your new life in the USA is really as great as you make it sound. You never seem to have any problems. It's great that you have friendly neighbours, but is this true for all of them? You should be a bit more honest about the challenges of living abroad. This would make your blogpost more realistic and more interesting to read – for me at least. – **Markus**

Dear Markus! Thanks for taking the time to comment on my post. Could I just say that I do mention some of the more difficult parts of living abroad in this post. For example, how difficult it can be to explore my neighbourhood on foot. I try to keep a balance between being positive about life in the USA and being realistic about its challenges.

b Read Ellie's post again. Are the sentences true (T) or false (F)? Correct the false sentences.

		T	F
1	Reading Ellie's post has made Natalya curious to find out about her experiences in the USA.	☐	☐
2	Ellie thinks that it's hard to remember American words, even if you hear them every day.	☐	☐
3	Sam would like to spend time in the USA at the end of this year.	☐	☐
4	Ellie considered living on her own before she decided to stay with a host family.	☐	☐
5	Markus wrongly claims that Ellie doesn't mention any difficulties in her blogpost.	☐	☐
6	Ellie replies to Markus that she tries to focus more on the positive things that happen to her and pay less attention to the negative things.	☐	☐

c Read these sentences from the comments and replies. Write 'S' next to the sentences where the gerund is the subject. Write 'O' next to the sentences where the gerund is the object.

☐ 1 **Learning** about your experiences in the USA is extremely interesting.

☐ 2 **Getting used to** new words for everyday things isn't always easy.

☐ 3 **Reading** them on the bus to school makes time go by a lot faster!

☐ 4 I've started **planning** my year abroad in the USA next year.

☐ 5 Would you recommend **staying** with a host family?

☐ 6 However, I can't help **asking** myself if your new life in the USA is really as great as you make it sound.

d Complete this new comment on Ellie's blog with the correct form of the verbs from the box.

do ■ empty ■ find out ■ help ■ learn ■ meet ■ read ■ sweep ■ work ■ write

Hi Ellie! I love ______________ (1) your blog! Thank you for sharing your experiences with us. ______________ (2) honestly about your life on a blog is never easy – I've tried it myself. I enjoy ______________ (3) about your everyday life in the USA as well as about your trips to places like Boston. Nobody likes ______________ (4) chores such as ______________ (5) the porch and ______________ (6) the dishwasher, but ______________ (7) your host family is clearly important and ______________ (8) with Nina and Alex sounds like fun! ______________ (9) new people sounds easy, which is good news. And ______________ (10) American English is clearly a must – I'll have to do some homework before I come to the USA.

Cat

Practice: Away from home

2 Sending text messages at the supermarket

a Read Ellie's text message to a friend in Scotland and change the American English words to British English words.

Hi! I'm just **standing in line** (1) at the supermarket and I was thinking of you. Do you remember that time when you bought those bright yellow **sneakers** (2)? There's someone standing in front of me with a very similar pair! I remember people turning to look at you as you were walking along the **sidewalk** (3), then one of them crashed into a **garbage** (4) container. I'm glad he didn't hurt himself!

1 ______________________

2 ______________________

3 ______________________

4 ______________________

b Read Ellie's text message to a friend in Lexington and change the British English words to American English words.

Hey there! Sorry for not replying sooner. I had a problem with my **mobile phone** (5). I think it's because I dropped it in the **garden** (6) this morning. I took it to the **toilet** (7) straight away and washed the dirt off in the sink. Now it seems to be OK again. It's a good thing my **mum** (8) isn't here or she'd be angry at me for not being more careful.

5 ______________________

6 ______________________

7 ______________________

8 ______________________

3 While I was doing my chores.

Some interesting things happened to Ellie while she was doing her chores. Complete the sentences with the past progressive form of the verbs in brackets.

1 While I ______________________ (*sweep*) the porch, I saw a rainbow in the sky.

2 While Alex and I ____________________________ (*work*) in the garden, it started to rain so we went back inside.

3 I ___________________________ (*not expect*) to see a cat on top of the bin when I took the rubbish out.

4 We ___________________________ (*play*) loud music, so we could still hear it with the vacuum cleaner on.

5 I ___________________________ (*not play*) with the dog, but he came to watch me empty the dishwasher.

6 When Vivian came round yesterday, she was surprised that I ____________________ ________ (*tidy*) my bedroom and singing.

→ students' book, pages 16/17

4 **Feeling homesick.** What were Ellie and Vivian doing? Look at the pictures and complete the sentences with the verbs in the box. Use the simple past and past progressive in each sentence.

eat ■ meet ■ stand in line ■ start ■ not understand ■ watch

1

2

3

1 Ellie ______________________ to think about her mother back home while she ______________________ a friend and her mother together.

2 While Vivian ______________________, she ______________________ some new people.

3 While Ellie ______________________ at the supermarket, a woman started talking to her, but she ______________________ anything.

5 **Ellie writes a new blogpost.** Ellie writes another blog about her life in the USA. Complete her entry with the simple past or past progressive form of the verbs in the box.

be ■ comment ■ decide ■ find ■ look ■ make ■ read ■ realize ■ search ■ not spend ■ think

Hi everybody! While I ______________________ (1) your comments on my last blogpost, I ______________________ (2) that quite a lot of you are interested in spending time in the USA, too. So when I ______________________ (3) about what I should write about in my next blogpost, I ______________________ (4) on tips for students who want to spend a year in the USA. Let me start by telling you a story ... When my parents and I ______________________ (5) information about studying abroad online, we ______________________ (6) thousands of websites. While we ______________________ (7), it ______________________ (8) helpful to check if the website was connected to a well-known organization or if the website just wanted to sell something! We ______________________ (9) very much time on websites like that! I looked for personal stories from students abroad on social media. And the great thing was that while I ______________________ (10) on the posts of students in the USA, I ______________________ (11) my first friends there, and we still chat to each other today!

6 WRITING FOCUS: My home region

a Ashley is a 14-year-old girl from the USA. Listen to her. She is talking about her region. Tick (✓) the name.

- ☐ The Southeast
- ☐ The Northeast
- ☐ The Midwest

b Listen again and make notes about Ashley's region.

1	Weather and climate	
2	Cities	
3	Sights and tourist attractions	
4	Food	
5	Sports teams	

c Now make a copy of the table above and think about the region in Germany where you live. Make notes about your region in the table.

d Use your notes from **c** to write a report about your town or region (120 – 150 words). Include an interesting fact about your region which other students might not know and add photos or pictures to your report.

New England: Birthplace of America

7 The Liberty Bell

a Look at the photo of the Liberty Bell. Why do you think this bell is so important in the history of the USA? Compare your ideas with a partner.

b Read the text and check if your prediction from **a** was correct.

The bell that changed history: The story of the Liberty Bell

For those who are not familiar with American history and the country's struggle for independence from the British in the 18th century, the Liberty Bell looks just like any other old bell. However, there is a reason why millions of people pay the admission to see it each year and that is its symbolic importance. It was in the Pennsylvania State House that the Declaration of Independence was signed on 2nd August 1776.

Prior to the Declaration, the bell had already been in place in the State House for 24 years. It had been produced in London and brought to the USA in 1752. The bell was cast with a verse from the bible on it which read: 'Proclaim LIBERTY Throughout All the Land Unto All the Inhabitants Thereof' – hence the name it's known by today. Originally, the bell was rung to tell lawmakers to come to the State House and to let the citizens of Philadelphia know about important announcements.

However, the Liberty Bell could not have been rung on 4th July 1776 when the vote for independence was taken because no immediate announcement of the decision was made. Most historians believe that the Liberty Bell was one of the bells rung four days later when the United States Declaration of Independence was publicly read. Yet, it would be almost another hundred years before the bell became famous. Campaigners for a ban on slavery used the bell as a symbol for their struggle for liberty in the 1840s and 1850s, and it became a symbol of hope and freedom in American popular culture.

The Liberty Bell's fame continued to grow during the rest of the 19th century and it travelled by train to seven different exhibitions and events around the USA. In 1948, control of the bell was transferred to the federal government who assigned it protected status. It was moved from City Hall to a specially designed glass pavilion in the 1970s so that it could be viewed more easily, and then to the Liberty Bell Center in 2003, where it stands to this day. Here, it is accompanied by an exhibition about the War of Independence and the Declaration of Independence. The Liberty Bell's symbolism remains strong and potent to this day – it seems that the message that mankind's liberty is something to be preserved and celebrated will never grow old.

c Read the text again and do the tasks.

1 Name the location which has contributed to the importance of the Liberty Bell.

______________________________.

2 Point out what feature of the bell is connected to the idea of liberty.

____

______________________________.

3 Outline the Liberty Bell's original purpose.

____

____.

4 Which movement in American history led to the increasing importance of the Liberty Bell?

____.

5 Outline the reason for the federal government's decision to move the bell to different locations.

____

____.

8 Old World Wisconsin

3 **a** Listen to Caitlin, a costume guide at Old World Wisconsin, talking to visitors. Number the things she does in the correct order.

- ☐ **a** thanks the visitors for coming to the museum
- ☐ **b** checks visitors have understood her talk
- ☐ **c** welcomes the visitors to the museum
- ☐ **d** tells them what they can expect from this talk
- ☐ **e** introduces herself

3 **b** Listen again and complete the tasks in your exercise book.

1 Explain what Caitlin does to get the visitors' attention.
2 Describe what she does to help the visitors understand what information she's going to give them.
3 Write what Caitlin says to check the visitors understand her and to invite them to ask her questions.

9 Neudegger Living History Museum

a Imagine that you are a costume guide at a living history museum. Read the notes and prepare your talk. Take turns to give your talk to a partner and listen to your partner's talk.

b Give each other feedback. Check whether your partner:

- got your attention at the beginning of his / her talk.
- helped you understand what information he / she was going to give you.
- made sure you understood and invited you to ask questions.

<u>Name and location of the museum:</u>
Neudegger Living History Museum, North Rhine Westphalia
<u>Attractions at the museum:</u>
thirty-two buildings showing life in the Rhine area over the last four centuries
<u>What visitors can learn about at the museum:</u>
what life was like in small rural communities on the Rhine in the past; the changing architecture in rural communities over time; the arts and handicrafts that the people of the Rhine have created.

Practice: Where it began

10 **Hamilton!** Ellie goes to watch the musical *Hamilton* in New York with her host family. Underline the relative clauses in each sentence.

Rapping the Revolution

Hello everyone! In my history class we have been learning about the American War of Independence, which is a very important war in American history. Sometimes I find learning about history a little boring because it is hard to imagine something that happened so long ago. This time, however, was different because last week we saw the Broadway musical *Hamilton*, which was amazing. It has totally changed how I think about history!

Hamilton is a musical about a man called Alexander Hamilton, who was one of the Founding Fathers of the United States. He had a really interesting life. He was born in the Caribbean and then came to America where he eventually became the country's first secretary of the treasury. In the musical, the events of his life are told through rap and hip-hop music, which is full of life and energy. The actors who perform in the musical are really talented.

Rap music and American history may seem like a strange combination, but it really works! Now that I've seen the events from the American Revolution in front of me, I can understand what really happened, and the rap music made me realize that the people back then were just like you and me. The musical has inspired me to learn more about our history and create some raps of my own that I can perform in our music class.

11 **The Boston Tea Party.** Look at the text and decide where the missing information from the box belongs. Rewrite the text. Be careful with commas.

which was called the Tea Act ■ which contained 90,000 pounds of tea ■ which was a very popular drink in Britain and the colonies ■ which was British ■ which took place in 1773 ■ who dressed as Native Americans ■ who refused to pay ■ who were angry

The Boston Tea Party * (1) was a political protest by the 'Sons of Liberty'. This is what happened. Tea * (2) made a lot of money for the East India Trading company. The colonies had to buy tea from this one company * (3). They were also told they had to pay high taxes on the tea * (4). The Americans * (5) demanded that the tea was sent back. When it wasn't, they decided to protest and throw the tea into the sea. However, nobody is quite sure if the destruction of the tea was planned or if some colonists * (6) destroyed it spontaneously. The protesters * (7) entered three ships in the harbor, and threw 342 containers * (8) into the sea! Today, that would be worth a million dollars.

12 An email to a friend

a Ellie visits Plimoth Plantation, a living history museum. Read the email she wrote to a friend in Scotland about her trip. Complete the email with the words from the box.

when ■ where ■ which/that ■ who ■ whose

Hi!

We visited the Plimoth Plantation in Plymouth, Massachusetts at the weekend. It's a really cool living museum ____________ (1) you can experience the life of the first European settlers ____________ (2) came to the USA in the 17th century. They've re-built the village so it looks the same as it did at the time ____________ (3) the first settlers were living there. We walked around the village and talked to the guides in period costumes ____________ (4) knowledge of life in 17th century Plymouth – or Plimoth – was excellent. My favourite part was the farm ____________ (5) had chickens and goats. I helped one of the guides to chop wood at the farm and we cooked one of the chickens over an open fire!

Have you ever been to an open-air museum like Plimoth Plantation?

Talk to you soon, Ellie

b Re-write the two sentences as one sentence with a relative pronoun.

1 I talked to one of the guides at the museum. She was wearing a period costume.

____

____.

2 She told us a story about the earliest settlers. Their descendants still live in the area.

____

____.

3 We learned about the 17th century. The first European settlers came to New England then.

____

____.

4 We visited a reservation. Native Americans have lived there for thousands of years.

____

____.

5 Our guide showed us some ancient tools. Native Americans used these tools.

____

____.

13 LISTENING FOCUS: William Penn

a Look at the picture. Speculate what this man achieved and tick (✓) the correct answers. Give reasons for your choice.

- ☐ 1 He was a military leader who fought the English in colonial America.
- ☐ 2 He was a religious man who wanted religious freedom.
- ☐ 3 He was a politician who made laws in colonial America.
- ☐ 4 He established a new colony in America.

4 **b** Listen to the story of William Penn and check your answers to **a**.

4 **c** Listen again and answer these questions.

1 Where was William Penn born?

______________________________.

2 What did you learn about William Penn's education?

______________________________.

3 What change happened in William Penn's life when he was 22 years old?

______________________________.

4 How did Penn's father feel about his religious beliefs at the beginning, and later on?

______________________________.

5 Why did Penn decide to leave England?

______________________________.

6 What did King Charles II give Penn and what is it called today?

______________________________.

d Look at these words from the text. Match them with their definitions.

1	chaos	a	a large amount of money
2	refuse	b	a situation where there is no order and nobody knows what's happening
3	capture	c	a pattern of lines that cross each other to make squares
4	fortune	d	not to do something that somebody else wants you to do
5	grid	e	catch

e Describe how you think William Penn felt when he left England and went to America to establish a new colony. Outline what challenges you think he had to face. Write about 150 words.

____

____

____

____

______________________________.

Internet research

14 Find and evaluate sources

a Imagine you need to find out information about American hero Ida Bell Wells-Barnett (more commonly known as Ida B. Wells) for a school history project. You want to find answers to these questions:

- Where and when was she born?
- What jobs or roles did she have?
- What did she achieve?
- What is she famous for?
- What is her legacy? What did she inspire later generations to do?

IDA B. WELLS.

Make a list of keywords you can use to search for this information about Ida B. Wells online.

My keywords:

____

____

____

b Make a list of five websites where you can find information about Ida B. Wells. Tick (✓) the websites that you think contain reliable, appropriate and useful information. If you can't tick three reliable websites, search again until you can.

	Website	reliable	unreliable
1		☐	☐
2		☐	☐
3		☐	☐
4		☐	☐
5		☐	☐

c Choose the three websites you ticked in **b** and write the details for these sources. What is useful, what isn't useful? Give reasons for your choice.

My chosen sources

1 reliable / useful: ______________________________

unreliable / not useful: ______________________________

2 reliable / useful: ______________________________

unreliable / not useful: ______________________________

3 reliable / useful: ______________________________

unreliable / not useful: ______________________________

→ students' book, pages 24/25

A nation of immigrants

15 The Bremerhaven Emigrants

a Leon visited the German Emigration Center in Bremerhaven with his class. He wrote a report about it for his teacher. Read Leon's report and answer the questions.

1 What is emigration?
2 What types of objects can you see at the German Emigration Center Bremerhaven?
3 What can you do there?

Last week, we visited the German Emigration Center in Bremerhaven. We'd learned about what happened to immigrants when they arrived in the USA, but I didn't know much about how immigrants left Europe and travelled to the USA. At the museum, we learned that 'emigrants' are people who leave their home country to go and live in another country, so 'emigration' means leaving your home country.

I didn't realize that so many Germans, and people from other European countries, boarded ships to New York in Bremerhaven in the 19th and 20th centuries. Seven million people did this between 1830 and 1974. During the time when people were emigrating to the USA from Bremerhaven, some were experiencing persecution in Europe, and there was often famine, which meant that people had very little to eat. But the emigrants who had these difficult lives were also people like us with mothers and fathers, brothers and sisters. They wanted to fall in love, have adventures and contribute to their country.

We saw some of the things they took with them on their journey. I remember clearly that we saw an old brush for brushing the hair of a horse. We read that it belonged to Martha Hüner, who was 17 years old when she emigrated to the USA in 1923. Her father gave her the brush because he thought she would marry an American cowboy. I can't imagine saying goodbye to my parents and going to live in another country at that age! We later found out that Martha married a baker. She didn't find great wealth in the USA, but she was happy.

We also explored a ship that took emigrants to the USA during the 1850s and 1860s, and we went to the research centre where you can search international databases to find family members who emigrated from Bremerhaven. I didn't find any members of my family, but my friend Luisa found some information about her great-great-great aunt!

b Find words in the text that math these definitions.

1 being treated badly because of your race or beliefs ______________________
2 not having enough food for a long time ______________________
3 to help to make something better or stronger ______________________
4 a large amount of money ______________________

c Work with a partner. Answer the questions.

1 What would you be most interested in at the German Emigration Center? Why?
2 Choose four objects you own that would show people in the future what your life is like today. Explain your choices.

16 An interview with an immigration advisor

5 **a** Burçu is an immigration advisor in New York. She helps immigrants to the USA to start a new life there. Listen to the interview with Burçu. Tick (✓) the things that she says she does in her job as an immigration advisor.

- [ ] 1 Reads information that clients give her about themselves.
- [ ] 2 Meets with clients face-to-face to give them advice.
- [ ] 3 Gives information about clients to the American government.
- [ ] 4 Has telephone conversations with clients to give them advice.
- [ ] 5 Visits clients' homes to make sure they can do everyday tasks like putting the garbage out on the correct day.
- [ ] 6 Explains to clients how to fill in paperwork.

5 **b** Listen again and make notes for these questions. Discuss your answers with a partner.

1 Why did Burçu decide to become an immigration advisor?

____

______________________________.

2 What are the three steps that Burçu goes through when she works with a client?

____

______________________________.

3 What does the length of time that Burçu works with a client depend on?

______________________________.

4 What does she advise all immigrants to do before they come and when they arrive?

____

______________________________.

c Imagine that you want to move to the USA. Write three questions you would like to ask Burçu.

1 ______________________________?
2 ______________________________?
3 ______________________________?

d Work with a partner. Read your partner's questions and write answers to them. Do some research online to find the answers if you need to. Then tell your partner the answers.

Practice: The American Dream

17 The French Quarter in New Orleans

a Read the article about the French Quarter in New Orleans, Louisiana and complete it with *a*, *the* or no article. Write *0* if no word is needed.

The French Quarter is probably __________ (1) most famous part of New Orleans. It was built by __________ (2) architects working for the French rulers of __________ (3) Louisiana in the 18th century, and the French Quarter's streets are named after French royal houses (Bourbon Street) or Catholic saints (St. Peter's Street). __________ (4) Quarter's architecture is typical of French colonial architecture with its galleries and balconies. __________ (5) French were in control of this area until the United States government paid $18 million to buy it from them in 1803. __________ (6) English-speaking Americans, who moved into New Orleans at that time, built houses on __________ (7) other side of town so the French Quarter's architecture didn't change. In fact, it was in the decades after the so-called 'Louisiana Purchase' that the Quarter's famous iron galleries were built on __________ (8) first floor of many buildings.

Unfortunately, the French Quarter fell into decline during the late 19th century and in the 1960s, __________ (9) highway was planned between the Mississippi Levee and the French Quarter, which would have produced a lot of noise and air pollution. However, the plans were never carried out because of the efforts of campaigners and __________ (10) new national historical buildings preservation law called the highway plan which was made in 1969. Today, the French Quarter is thriving again, after the damage caused to New Orleans by __________ (11) Hurricane Katrina in 2005. It is now known for its long history, Cajun food, and its annual Mardi Gras celebration where thousands of people in costumes celebrate on __________ (12) streets.

>>> **b** Think of a place in Germany (or another country you have visited) where you can see and experience life through its architecture, food and culture. Write a paragraph of about 80 – 100 words to describe this place.

____

____

____

____

____

18 German towns in Texas

a Read the article about German towns in Texas from a website for tourists. Complete the text with *a*, *the* or no article. Write *0* if no word is needed.

☐ When you think of ________________ (1) Texas, you probably think of a cowboy riding a horse and it may seem like the most typically 'American' place. ________________ (2) reality is that there is a lot of diversity there. Did you know that the largest European ethnic group in the state of Texas is German? The great-great grandparents of today's German Texans founded many beautiful towns in ________________ (3) Texas Hill Country which you can visit on ________________ (4) trip to Texas today.

☐ Every German Texan town has older buildings with ________________ (5) German architecture that were built over 150 years ago. You may also hear people saying words from Texas German. This is ________________ (6) type of old German that was spoken by descendants of the original German settlers. Nobody has spoken Texas German as their first language since the 1970s, but some people will still mix Texas German with ________________ (7) English. However, the easiest way to know if you're in a Texas German town is probably by ________________ (8) town's name. They often end in *-berg*, *-burg*, *-ingen* or *-ens*, like German towns do.

☐ Fredericksburg is ________________ (9) pretty German Texan town located about an hour and a half outside of San Antonio. The town was founded in 1846 and its German founders wanted to show their respect for Prince Frederick of Prussia when they chose its name. There are about 50 wineries and vineyards in ________________ (10) town of Fredericksburg and the countryside around it. Tourists can see how the wine is made and try ________________ (11) glass themselves.

☐ One year older than Fredericksburg, New Braunfels is better known than any other German Texan town. Its historic buildings are even on ________________ (12) National Register of Historic Places. You'll find most of these historic buildings in ________________ (13) Gruene region of the town where there are a lot of boutique shops and restaurants. But how can you be sure that this is ________________ (14) German town? A beer festival is held every year, but it isn't called Oktoberfest, it's called Wurstfest instead.

b Read the article again. Match the headings with the paragraphs.

A The most famous German Texan town
B The town named after a prince
C Beautiful German towns you need to visit in Texas
D How do you know you're in a German town?

»» **c** Do some internet research about German towns in Texas. Imagine visiting one. Write a postcard to a friend. Tell him / her:

- What the buildings in the town are like.
- What you can see and do in the town.
- If you heard any local people speaking Texans German.
- What you think about the town.

19 SPEAKING FOCUS: Describing and interpreting photos

a Work with a partner and look at the two photos. Say where you think each photo was taken and explain why you think so.

b Brainstorm words for the things you can see in each photo.

A

B

c What are the similarities and differences between the two photos? Make notes in a table.

Similarities	Differences

d Tell your partner which place you would prefer to visit and explain why.

e Use the phrases in the box to compare the photos. Give your opinion about which place is more interesting for tourists in the USA to visit.

Compare the photos.
Both photos ...
In this photo, the people are ..., while in this one ...

Make guesses about the situation.
The people in this photo look ...
It looks as if they are ...

Give your opinion.
I think ...
In my opinion, ...

Going west

20 A school project

a Ellie is researching the Oregon Trail for a school project. She found a blog written by someone who drove the trail on her own. Complete the diary with verbs in the correct form.

Traveling along the Oregon Trail

Day 1: I ____________________ (1) my journey in Kansas City, Missouri. I ____________________ (2) there by train and when we arrived it was 9 p.m. and the sun ____________________ (3) down, so I couldn't see the city very well. I ____________________ (4) up my hire car and then checked into the hotel.

Day 2: Today, I ____________________ (5) 20 miles to Independence, Missouri to visit the National Frontier Trails Museum there. I ____________________ (6) online that this museum ____________________ (7) really interesting because it tells the story of the pioneers who ____________________ (8) westwards on the Oregon Trail in the 19th century.

Day 3: It ____________________ (9) time to leave Missouri behind me and get a feel for life on the trail. Traveling towards Kearney, Nebraska, I ____________________ (10) the car a few times to get out and look at graves on the side of the road. These were the graves of people who ____________________ (11) on the trail long ago.

Day 4: After spending the night in Kearney, I ____________________ (12) on driving until I got to Lewellen, Nebraska. The drive ____________________ (13) very interesting, but Lewellen has a great trading post.

b Ellie has now written the introduction to her Oregon Trail project. She has made some mistakes. Read the text and decide whether the underlined parts are correct or not. Tick (✓) the correct ones and correct the wrong ones.

<u>I'm really liking</u>[1] the stories of people who <u>was involved</u>[2] in the migration westwards. I remember <u>that I read</u>[3] about two <u>familys</u>[4] who planned to go to Oregon to start a new <u>live</u>[5], but <u>didn't make</u>[6] it. Their whole group <u>were becoming ill</u>[7] and <u>died of</u>[8] the same mysterious illness. I also read a story about <u>a herd of bisons</u>[9] that roamed across the plains <u>one day</u>[10] and saw some pioneers who had lost their way on the trail. <u>Amazing</u>[11], the herd showed the pioneers the way back to the trail. There was a family who <u>took</u>[12] a herd of <u>sheeps</u>[13] with them on their journey. <u>Much of them</u>[14] didn't survive the long journey, but some of them arrived in Oregon <u>safely</u>[15].

21 The creation of the reservations

a You are going to listen to an expert talking about the impact that American political institutions have had on the lives of Native Americans. Before you listen, read her notes for the talk. Then listen and tick (✓) the points that she talks about.

Background

☐ **Goals of reservations:**
- control
- less conflict
- live more like the white population

☐ **History:**
- 1785 – Treaty of Hopwell
- early 19th century – moving Native Americans from the Southeast
- 1830 – the Indian Removal Act
- next few years – the Trail of Tears

The creation of the reservations

☐ **Legal background:**
- 1851 – Congress passed the Indian Appropriations Act
- 1887 – the Dawes Act, signed by President Grover Cleveland, divided reservations
- 1934 – the Dawes Act replaced by the Indian Reorganization Act

☐ **Effects on Native Americans:**
- harder to keep culture and traditions
- conflict between different nations
- change in family life

Reservations today

☐ **Social situation**
- 22 % of Native Americans on reservations
- almost 30 % are poor
- work for their nation's government or the federal government
- 4 – 8 out of 10 = not working
- housing = often not big enough

☐ **The economy**
- lack of economic opportunity
- biggest sources of income are from tourism and gambling
- government money is still needed – often not enough available

b Listen to the talk and read the notes again. Then complete the tasks.

1 Outline the reasons for setting up the reservations.
2 Explain the role of the American government in the establishment of the reservations.
3 Describe the impact of the reservations on Native Americans' daily life.
4 Comment on what you think the American government should do to improve the quality of life of Native Americans who live on reservations.

c Work with a partner and role-play an interview with the expert on Native American reservations. Prepare some questions and then use the notes to give answers.

Practice: This land is our land

22 The beautiful Southwest

a Zoe, a student from the UK, visited the Southwest of the USA with her family. Listen to her presentation about the trip and decide if the sentences are true (T) or false (F). Correct the false sentences.

		T	F
1	Zoe thinks her class already knows a lot about the Southwest.	☐	☐
	____.		
2	It's very hot in the Southwest all year round.	☐	☐
	____.		
3	Zoe experienced temperatures of over 40 degrees during her trip.	☐	☐
	____.		
4	There are large parts of the Southwest where nobody lives.	☐	☐
	____.		
5	The cities in the Southwest are quite different to other cities in the USA.	☐	☐
	____.		
6	Zoe went on a boat trip along the river at the Grand Canyon.	☐	☐
	____.		
7	Zoe wasn't very familar with New Mexico before the trip.	☐	☐
	____.		

b Read the extracts from the diary that Zoe wrote during her trip. Then complete the sentences with the correct form of the verb in brackets.

A summer holiday in the Southwest

Day 1

We ______________________ (1) (*fly*) from London Heathrow Airport to Phoenix, Arizona this morning. I ______________________ (2) (*never be*) on such a long flight until today. We ______________________ (3) (*fly*) for about six hours before the pilot told us that we were flying above the United States!

Day 3

My jet lag seems to have gone now and we ______________________ (4) (*have*) a great day in Phoenix today. The city is like the typical American city that

I ________________________________ (5) (*imagine*) before we came here. There are lots of big shopping malls and palm trees on the pavements, or sidewalks as they are called here!

Day 7

Today, we __________________________ (6) (*visit*) the Grand Canyon, which was amazing. I ___________________________________ (7) (*not realize*) that nature could be so beautiful. It's almost impossible to describe how awesome it is – you have to experience it for yourself.

Day 9

Early this morning, we __________________________ (8) (*get*) into our hire car and drove into New Mexico. I ____________________________________ (9) (*not know*) very much about this part of the world this morning, but now I'm learning more about the wonderful New Mexico landscapes!

23 **Pioneer ancestors.** Jaden and his mother have been researching their family tree. Circle the correct verb forms to complete their conversation about their ancestors.

Jaden — So tell me more about my great-great-great-great-grandparents, Mom.

Mom — Well, they **were/had been** (1) pioneers, Jaden. They **set off/had set off** (2) from Missouri in 1865 and travelled westwards to Wyoming – that's a very long distance to travel.

Jaden — How **did they travel/had they been travelling** (3)?

Mom — They **travelled/had been travelling** (4) in a wagon train, so there were always other families in front of and behind them, and they could help each other to cope with the difficult conditions on the trail.

Jaden — I **hadn't realized/hadn't been realizing** (5) they took animals with them until I read that one family of pioneers took a lot of cows.

Mom — Well, I'm not sure if anyone took a lot of cows with them. Maybe just three or four.

Jaden — Did the pioneers look like those people you see dressed in period costumes at living history museums?

Mom — Probably. But remember they **didn't own/hadn't owned** (6) many clothes and some pioneers **had/had been travelling** (7) for over a year when they reached Oregon.

Jaden — I think all the descendants of the people who travelled along the Oregon Trail should make an effort to find out more about their stories – like we're doing.

Mom — When I started my research, our family **had lost/had been losing** (8) a lot of documents, but there's some good information online that will help us.

24 READING FOCUS: A letter to the editor

a This text is a letter to the editor of a US newspaper. Read the text and answer the questions.

1 Who is the writer? ______________________.

2 What did she read in the newspaper that inspired her to write this letter?

______________________.

3 Why does the writer have a problem with what she read in last week's newspaper?

____

______________________.

4 What does the writer want to happen in future?

____

______________________.

Dear editor,

I was very upset to see some statistics in last week's newspaper which showed how Americans voted and organized them into the following ethnic groups: White, Black, Hispanic, Asian and Other. As a Native American, I imagine that my people – the original settlers in this country – are so unimportant to your newspaper that you cannot even use the name of our ethnic group.

In my opinion, including Native Americans in public discussions about politics is a particularly important issue because not enough Native Americans come out to vote. There are many reasons for this. Native Americans often trust their local and national government less than other ethnic groups. They often don't have enough information about how to register to vote, and they usually live far away from the places where they can do this. This is usually due to the fact that Native Americans are less likely to have internet access and many of them live on reservations.

Past governments of the USA have tried to pretend that Native Americans do not exist. They have shown no respect for the land they live on, for example, by allowing the Dakota Access Pipeline project in the Midwest. However, it is now the responsibility of the media to show both Native Americans and all other Americans that we live in this country, too, and we also have the right to take part in its politics. Therefore, I would ask you to remember to include us in your future statistics and news articles instead of using the word 'Other' which, sounds like we are not welcome in our own country.

Sharice Hyland

b What's the main argument of the text? Choose the statement that sums it up best.

☐ 1 The American government should make sure that more Native Americans become politicians.

☐ 2 The media needs to include Native Americans in their reports about politics.

☐ 3 Projects like the Dakota Access Pipeline should stop because they take Native Americans' rights away.

Research, write and evaluate a short article

25 An informative article

a Ellie has written an informative article for her American classmates about a popular tourist destination in the UK. Read the different parts of the article and put them in the correct order (A – F).

☐ Six years and £134 million later, the Tate Modern was opened by the Queen. Much of the original structure of the building remained and a glass front was added to the roof. The gallery consists of a permanent exhibition of Tate's collection of 20th-century modern art and a range of temporary exhibitions featuring modern artists including Monet and Picasso.

☐ To sum up, Tate Modern is an excellent example of how old buildings can be turned into spaces where people can enjoy the arts, even if they wouldn't usually go to art exhibitions.

☐ Tate Modern: Bringing modern art to the masses in style

☐ Today, Tate Modern is well established as a 'must-see' attraction for tourists visiting London. It attracts both art lovers and non-art lovers and is particularly popular with families. Some people's main motivation for visiting Tate Modern is for the beautiful views of the city of London from the top of the building, with St Paul's Cathedral and the Millennium Bridge directly opposite it.

☐ Are you one of those people for whom the idea of looking at paintings in an art gallery sounds boring? If that's the case, many people with the same attitude as you have visited Tate Modern, one of London's top tourist attractions, and found that they were wrong. This art gallery presents exciting modern and contemporary art in a former power station and challenges our ideas about what going to an art exhibition is like.

☐ The building in which Tate Modern can be found was originally known as Bankside Power Station and it took 16 years before it was finally completed in 1963. Two decades later, in 1981, the power station closed. It was empty for many years and developers had even considered demolishing it. In 1994, the Tate Gallery announced that it would take over the building and redevelop it as a modern art gallery.

b Now evaluate Ellie's article. Use the checklist and make notes on your answers to the questions.

☐ Does the article have a clear structure?

☐ Does the writer use linking words to connect ideas, e. g. adding ideas: *and, also*; contrasting ideas: *but, although, however*; introducing causes and reasons: *so, because (of), as a result, that's why*; introducing examples: *for example, for instance*

☐ Is the grammar and spelling correct?

Mediation

26 Open-Air Museum Hagen

a Your partner school in the USA wants to make a newspaper on the wall to present museums in the countries of their partner schools. It's your job to write a text (about 150 words) about an interesting museum. During your last holidays, you got a brochure about the Open-Air Museum in Hagen. Use the brochure to write a text about this museum. Include information about where the museum is located and what visitors can see and do in this museum.

LWL-Freilichtmuseum Hagen

[...] Historische Maschinen, traditionell hergestellte Produkte, idyllische Natur – das LWL-Freilichtmuseum Hagen bietet viele Gründe für einen Besuch.

Über 50 Werkstätten und Betriebe, kilometerlange Spazierwege, drei Gastronomie-Betriebe, Spiel- und Erlebnisplätze, Einkaufsmöglichkeiten im Museumsshop – da fällt es schwer, sich zu entscheiden. [...]

[...] Das LWL-Freilichtmuseum Hagen liegt in einem wunderschönen langgestreckten Tal mit einigen Steigungen. Es präsentiert Gebäude und Werkstätten aus der Zeit vom Ende des 18. Jahrhunderts bis in die 1960er-Jahre.

Die Häuser und Werkstätten waren damals in der Regel eng, sie hatten steile Treppen und waren häufig nicht ebenerdig betretbar. Wir bauen solche Barrieren so weit wie möglich ab. Durch unsere speziellen Angebote möchten wir Menschen mit unterschiedlichsten Einschränkungen einen schönen Aufenthalt in unserem eindrucksvollen Museum ermöglichen. [...]

In einigen Museumsbereichen ist Kopfsteinpflaster verlegt, andere Wege sind mit wassergebundenem Belag versehen. Bei einigen Steigungen ist die Unterstützung durch eine Begleitperson notwendig. An mehreren Stellen im Museumsgelände haben wir neue zusätzliche Wege geschaffen, auf denen die Gebäude des Museums ohne Probleme erreicht werden können.

Ein Übersichtsplan für Menschen mit körperlichen Einschränkungen ist an der Eingangskasse kostenlos erhältlich.

Seilerei, Schmieden und Mühlen

Das Freilichtmuseum verbindet sinnliche Erfahrung mit Wissensgewinn. Das liegt vor allem an den vielen Werkstätten, in denen täglich geschulte Handwerkerinnen und Handwerker arbeiten und alte Techniken zeigen. Sie schmieden Nägel, rollen Zigarren, schlagen Seile und vermitteln andere, heute vielfach in Vergessenheit geratene Arbeitstechniken. Etwa achtzehn der rund 60 Werkstätten sind jeden Tag in Betrieb. [...]

→ students' book, pages 34/35

Allgemeine Informationen
Bei unseren Programmen und Führungen gehen wir gerne auf Bedürfnisse von Menschen mit körperlichen oder geistigen Einschränkungen ein.

Eine Broschüre über das Museum in leichter Sprache können Sie auf unserer Webseite herunterladen. In Kürze können wir Ihnen die Broschüre auch als barrierefreies PDF anbieten. [...]

[...] Sie dürfen im Museum gerne zu privaten Zwecken fotografieren oder filmen. Bitte benutzen Sie keinen Blitz oder andere künstliche Lichtquellen, wenn Sie unsere Handwerkerinnen und Handwerker bei der Arbeit fotografieren. [...]

www.lwl-freilichtmuseum-hagen.de

b Your partner school in the USA has some questions about the museum. You can answer some of these questions with the help of the brochure, but not all of them so you need to contact the museum. Write an email in which you ask the questions that you can't answer.

- How is the museum financed?
- Can visitors take photos in the museum?
- Are there any animals in the museum?
- What does LWL stand for?
- Can visitors help the craftsmen and women?
- How about visitors in a wheelchair? Can they visit the museum, too?

Guten Tag, ______

My review

1 About chores

1 taking out
2 rubbish
3 chore
4 doing
5 cleaning
6 vacuuming
7 Walking
8 sweeping
9 yard
10 bin
11 emptying
12 dishwasher

2 About life in the past

1 hard life
2 one-room
3 tidying
4 emptying
5 heating
6 open fire
7 chopping wood
8 fetching water
9 grew
10 vegetables
11 keeping
12 hunting

3 About national holidays and celebrations

1 declared
2 had been fighting
3 did the war finish
4 carried on
5 had been collecting
6 threw
7 didn't make
8 didn't become

4 About immigration

1 the
2 0
3 the
4 the
5 0
6 0
7 0
8 a
9 a
10 0
11 0
12 0
13 0

Making friends

1 **New people.** Conor O'Brien is an Irish student in Charleston, South Carolina. Complete the sentences about Conor's new life with verbs in the present perfect or present perfect progressive and add *for* and *since*.

1 Conor ______________________________ (*be*) at West Ashley High School __________ some months now and he __________________________ (*make*) some friends.

2 He ___________________________________ (*play*) in the school band ______________ the beginning of October.

3 He ____________ also _________________ (*meet*) Alisha and Meg. Jordan ______________________________ (*tell*) Conor that Meg is very talented. She knows a lot about music because she ___________________________________ (*listen*) to jazz all her life.

4 Meg's father is a jazz musician. He ___________________________________ (*perform*) at jazz concerts ________ more than 40 years. Conor is excited because he ______________________________ (*never meet*) anyone whose father is a jazz musician.

2 **Conor.** Two girls are talking about Conor. Complete their conversation with the present perfect or present perfect progressive and one of these words: *already*, *for*, *since*, *yet*. Remember the word order in questions.

A ___________________________________ (1) (*you/meet*) Conor, ________________ (2)?

B Yes. He ________________________________ (3) (*play*) in our band _____________ (4) a few weeks now.

A How long ___________________________________ (5) (*he/be*) here?

B _________________ (6) the beginning of the school year, so _________________ (7) September.

A It seems he ___________________________________ (8) (*make*) a few friends.

B Yes, I ____________________________ (9) (*see*) him with Jordan in the cafeteria …

3 8 **Jazz on the beach.** It's Sunday afternoon and Conor, Jordan and Alisha are at a concert on Folly Beach. Listen to Alisha and Jordan and summarize their conversation using the present perfect and present perfect progressive.

4 Teen life

a Complete this article with the correct form of the verbs from the box.

become ■ do ■ hang out ■ listen ■ look after ■ look for ■ make ■ start ■ take care ■ take part ■ volunteer ■ not want

What is it like to be a young person in the United States?

American children typically ____________________ (1) school when they are four or five years old and this is where they spend the next 12 years of their lives. Of course, as well as formal learning, many students ____________________ (2) in sports and cultural activities both at school and in their free time.

Nearly all teens love ____________________ (3) to music or ____________________ (4) at a friend's, playing computer games or watching movies. However, most young people ____________________ (5) to be completely dependent on their parents. That's why many young Americans ____________________ (6) a part-time job after school or at weekends, for example working in a fast food restaurant or ____________________ (7) the neighbours' kids. Of course, some students ____________________ (8) the mistake of taking on too much work and then they don't have enough time ____________________ (9) their homework!

In the US, volunteering is believed to help young people ____________________ (10) responsible citizens. Nowadays, ____________________ (11) of the environment is an important issue so, as well as the more traditional charity work, more and more young Americans ____________________ (12) to help clean up their local surroundings.

b Compare your lifestyle with that of American teenagers. How similar or different is it?

5 A blogpost

9 **a** Listen to four students discussing a blogpost and note down what they talk about.

10 **b** Listen to the second part of the conversation and do the tasks.

1 Indicate the frequency with which Americans listen to music.
2 Explain what these results show.
3 Name America's favourite music genres. What differences does the study show?
4 Indicate how music listening has changed in the last few years and explain the reasons.

Practice: Media and entertainment

6 Free-time activities

a Think of the activities you do in your free time. Make notes about which are your favourite and how much time you spend on them during the week.

b Compare your answers with a partner. How similar or different are your results? What sort of activities do you do more often? What activities do you do less often?

7 A bar chart

a This chart shows what German young people do daily or weekly in their free time. Talk to your partner and discuss which activities from the box you think are done most or least often.

do sports ■ meet with friends ■ play outside ■ read a book ■ read comics ■ use mobile phone / smartphone ■ watch TV

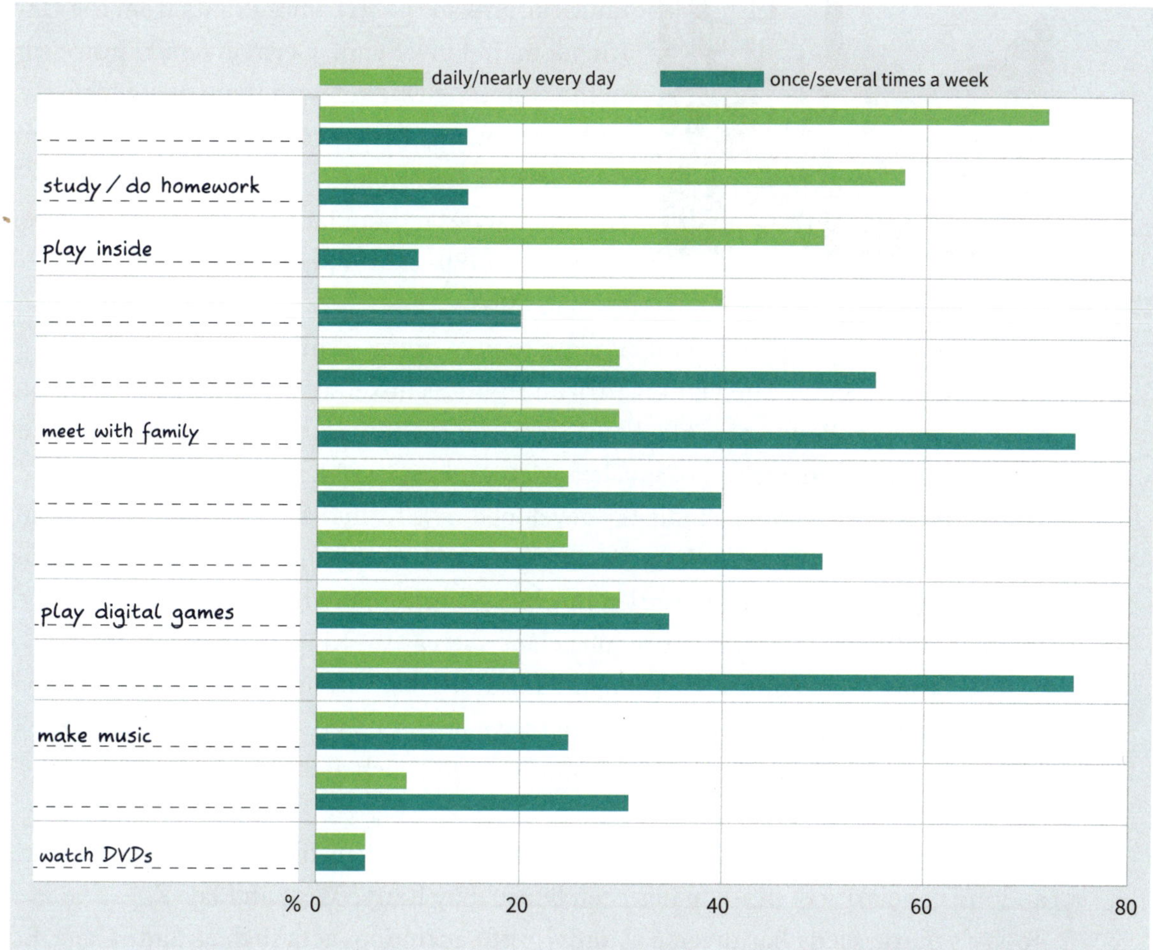

b Listen to a talk explaining the results of the survey. Complete the bar chart with the correct answers and compare them with yours. Comment on the similarities and differences.

→ students' book, pages 48/49

8 12 **Alisha's article.** Alisha has read an article online and is telling her friends about it. Listen and do the tasks.

1 Indicate what the article is about.
2 Explain who Marley Dias is and why she has become famous.
3 Explain what motivated her.
4 Outline why Rishab Jain is trying to find hospital and physician partners.
5 Describe how Jace Norman uses his popularity.

9 **Music, music, music!**

a Read the text and put phrases A–H in the correct place.

A has roots in the emergence of
B Here, it became blues as we know it
C In the 17th century
D Meanwhile, in Memphis
E has seen the rise of contemporary forms
F In the 20th century
G which came to include diverse styles
H inspired by music from the past

The music of the United States is influenced by many different cultures and reflects the country's multiculturalism. ☐ (1), immigrants from the United Kingdom, Ireland, Spain, Germany and France came to the country, bringing with them new music styles and instruments. African slaves also brought their own musical traditions.
Different styles of popular music started to appear early in the 19th century and much of modern American music ☐ (2) African American blues.
In those days, slaves gathered on Sundays to play drums, dance and sing in Congo Square, New Orleans. The vibrant African rhythms mixed with the sounds of Europe and created jazz. Performers like Louis Armstrong, Billie Holiday and John Coltrane have influenced generations of musicians around the world.
☐ (3), the American music industry developed new forms of music, using blues and other genres of American folk music. Between 1916 and 1970, large numbers of African Americans left the South and settled in Chicago, bringing with them the sounds of the Mississippi Delta. ☐ (4) thanks to musicians such as BB King or Muddy Waters.
☐ (5), during the recording of a song by Ike and Tina Turner, an accidental fault in an amplifier created a new guitar sound that gave birth to rock. In the 1960s and early 1970s, rock and roll changed into rock music, ☐ (6) such as surf, symphonic rock, heavy metal and punk.
The 21st century ☐ (7) of rhythm and blues through artists like Beyoncé and Rihanna, and the popularity of hip-hop has been boosted by Kanye West and Jay-Z.
Today's music scene has diverse sounds ☐ (8), including acts such as Lady Gaga, Ed Sheeran, Imagine Dragons and Greta Van Fleet.

b Underline the words you don't understand and look them up in a dictionary.

10 VIEWING FOCUS: A film trailer

1 2

a Watch the trailers for two films, then answer the questions and do the tasks.

1 What genre are they? Explain your choices.

____

____

2 Read this outline and decide which trailer it is about.

> This film is about a young man, the protagonist, and his neighbour with whom he has always had a romantic fascination. As adolescents they discover the body of a man who committed suicide. Some years later, she has become the most popular girl in school and he is an outcast. One night, a month before graduation, she tells her friend about her plan to take revenge on a group of people she feels hurt her during her time at high school, including her boyfriend, who cheated on her. That night the protagonist helps her carry out the plan and they return to their homes around dawn. The following morning she is reported missing by her family.

3 Outline the story of the other film as shown in the trailer.

____

____

____

____

4 In your opinion, how effective is each trailer? What makes you say that?

____

____

____

____

5 Would you recommend either of the films? Why or why not?

____

____

____

____

b How do you think the films will end? Explain your answers.

____

____

____

____

____

Shopping challenge

11 Generation gap

a An international online magazine has interviewed two siblings, Maia (M) and Otis (O) from different generations. Read the first part of the interview and do the tasks. Choose the correct words and phrases.

I Maia and Otis, you're siblings but you're from different generations. How does that feel? Are you very different?

M Well, I think so. But if we **were / would be** (1) the same, life **were / would be** (2) very boring! I belong to Generation Y – the millennials. I was born in 1995 and Otis is much younger.

O I'm 21, so I belong to Generation Z. I agree that in some ways we're different, but if you **asked / would ask** (3) me what's important to me now, it probably **won't be / wouldn't be** (4) very different from what you considered important **when / if** (5) you were my age.

I So how are you different from your sister's generation, Otis?

O We're very competitive. And **when / unless** (6) I say competitive, I **don't mean / won't mean** (7) just in sports. Our competitive nature applies to almost everything. We know that if we **don't work / won't work** (8) hard at school, we **don't get / won't get** (9) the good grades we need if we **want to / will** (10) get a place at college. My generation has also been shaped by the circumstances we were born into, which of course is true of all generations. If it **weren't / wouldn't be** (11) for terrorism, school shootings, environmental problems and the consequences of the economic crisis, perhaps many of us **won't be / wouldn't be** (12) so inspired to change the world. Most of us are socially aware and, if we have the chance, we **will do / would do** (13) our best to contribute, create, lead and learn.

I So you're quite idealistic?

O No, quite the opposite. We want to change the world but we're very practical. I think millennials are much more idealistic.

I What do you think, Maia?

M Well, if by idealistic you **mean / would mean** (14) chasing your dreams, then yes, we **would be / are** (15). We grew up during the economic boom with people telling us that we could be whatever we wanted. Many people my age are now starting their own businesses. But if we **work / will work** (16) for someone else, we **have / would have** (17) high expectations of our employers. We also look for new challenges at work and, although we respect authority, if we **don't agree / didn't agree** (18) with something, we aren't afraid to question it. We are also team players. My brother's generation is more individualistic.

b In your own words, summarize the differences between Generation Y and Generation Z as explained by Maia and Otis.

c Listen to the second part of the interview and write down the main topics that are mentioned.

____

____

____

d Listen again and complete the sentences.

1 When choosing jobs, Generation Z ____.

2 Financial stability is important for them because ____.

3 If they see an opportunity, ____.

4 Millennials would feel isolated if ____.

5 When face-to-face communication isn't available, Generation Z ____.

e Explain the meaning of these words and phrases as they are used in the interview.

1 compensation and benefits

____

2 financial stability

____

3 struggle during the crisis

____

4 isolated from the world

____

f Listen to the last part of the interview and explain how millennials and Generation Z differ in their shopping habits.

____

____

____

g Compare Otis's and Maia's views with your own and people your age. How similar or different are you? Write about it in your exercise book. Include sentences with *if*, *unless* and *when*.

→ students' book, pages 52/53

Practice: The cost of fast fashion

12 Fast fashion

a Read the blogpost that a student has written in reply to an interview with fashion design student Amy Rice. Put phrases A – L in the correct place.

A According to
B But at the same time
C by what's
D despite
E However
F I'd much rather
G If there is
H if we want to
I If you're young
J Like never before
K over and over again
L quite the opposite

☐ (1) one thing that defines Generation Z, it is that we're environmentally woke. ☐ (2) today's young people are collectively taking action to fight the climate crisis and we believe companies have a responsibility to address environmental and social issues. ☐ (3) when it comes to fashion, there is a contradiction in terms as we are environmentally engaged but tempted ☐ (4) new and fashionable.
We are not big spenders; ☐ (5), we are price-conscious and like to save money. ☐ (6), we love to shop and to show off on social media, ☐ (7) our reservations about the fashion industry. So brands have taken advantage of these traits to target their sales. ☐ (8), environmentally conscious, but don't have much money, fast fashion is just the thing for you!
Fast fashion brands produce at least one new 'collection' every week. Low-priced dresses, bikinis and bodysuits are made by factories at breakneck speed and their digital-first business model allows them to slash prices and use budgets for targeted marketing campaigns.
There's an unwritten but golden rule for us: you will not be seen in the same outfit ☐ (9) especially once it's available online. So my friends and I often swap clothes to avoid this, but with the staggeringly low cost of items available, it's easy to purchase a new outfit for every event, ☐ (10). For festivals, many of us stock up on new looks for those two or three days and then we never wear those clothes again. ☐ (11) Oxfam, the carbon footprint of new clothes bought each month in the US is greater than flying a plane around the world more than 900 times! We are certainly aware of fast fashion's environmental impact. I remember watching a show about fast fashion and how cotton is drying up areas of the world, and then feeling really guilty whenever I bought something. ☐ (12) make sure I'd turned off all my lights and stopped buying plastic water bottles … but clothes. Giving up fast fashion can require considerable willpower. What can I do?

b Find words in the text that match these definitions.

1 together as a group ______________________

2 to behave in a way that attracts attention and makes people admire you ______________

3 particular qualities in someone's character or personality ______________________

4 to greatly reduce costs ______________________

5 to give something to someone in exchange for something else ______________________

6 the ability to control your thoughts and behaviour in order to achieve something

____

c Summarize the main points of the article and explain the writer's position regarding fast fashion.

13 Less is more

a Complete this story about an interesting way to 'stand out from the crowd'.

Lots of young people my age think, 'If I ______________ (1) (*have*) more money, I ______________ (2) (*buy*) more clothes'. But I wouldn't. And why? Because I have a unique collection of the best clothes in town. Of course, if it ______________ (3) (*not be*) for Carla's Creations, that ______________ (4) (*not be*) the case. My mum is Carla and she is so creative. When I ______________ (5) (*see*) something I like on social media, I ______________ (6) (*show*) Mum and if she ______________ (7) (*have*) time, she ______________ (8) (*create*) something similar but better. Unless I ______________ (9) (*say*) I want a certain colour, she ______________ (10) (*choose*) and it always looks great. But, of course, it takes time. If I ______________ (11) (*go*) to the local mall for new clothes, it would be much quicker and I ______________ (12) (*have*) more in my wardrobe. But more clothes that looked like everyone else's. And that's the difference!

b Complete the following sentences by giving your opinions about fast fashion and the environment.

1 I would ______________ unless ______________________.

2 If I don't have money, ______________________.

3 If I had a few social events over a couple of weeks, I ______________________

______________________.

4 If I had to give up something to help protect the environment ______________________

______________________.

14 **Your reply.** Write your reply to the interview on page 52 of your students' book (150 – 200 words).

15 **SPEAKING FOCUS: A short talk about fast fashion**

a You have been asked to represent your school at a public speaking competition. You have chosen to speak about your generation's attitudes to shopping and fashion trends. Brainstorm ideas and make notes. Do some research or use ideas from the Workshop. Remember it is not necessary to write full sentences. Write as many ideas as you wish.

b Read your brainstorming notes and choose the ideas you find the most interesting.

c Structure your talk. How are you going to present your ideas in each section of the talk? Write down some useful expressions you can use.

d Organize your notes under each of the three headings.

- Introduction
- Middle
- Conclusion

e Write your talk.

Write a short questionnaire for a survey

16 **Brainstorm the topic.** You want to find out how interested in music students in your school are. Brainstorm questions for your survey.

17 **Write a first draft**

a Read the questions below and decide if they are good or bad survey questions. Explain why.

1 Do you take private music lessons? On what instrument? For how long?
☐ Yes ☐ No

2 How often do you listen to music?
☐ every day ☐ three times a week or more ☐ less than three times a week

3 What instrument would you like to play? ______________________

4 What's your favourite kind of music? Select all the options that apply.
☐ Rock ☐ Pop ☐ Rap ☐ Heavy metal ☐ Reggae ☐ Blues ☐ Jazz
☐ Classical ☐ Folk ☐ Other: ______________________

b Rewrite the bad questions.

____

____

____

18 **Write your questionnaire.** Use questions from **17** and your own to write a good questionnaire about students and music.

TIP

Remember:
1 Write short and simple questions.
2 Write questions that will give the exact answers you want.
3 Write questions that allow people to answer honestly.
4 Give enough options to choose from.

____

____

____

____

____

____

____

____

____

____

____

Going to school in the USA

19 An English boy in New Mexico

a Joshua has been in Santa Fe for some time now. What do you remember about his experiences? Complete these sentences with the correct form of the verbs in the box.

be ■ do ■ drive ■ get up ■ go ■ join ■ meet ■ see ■ sleep ■ take

1 Joshua enjoys ______________ an exchange student and he likes ______________ people from different cultures.

2 He hates ______________ early because he usually goes to bed late. Maybe he should try ______________ to bed earlier because he definitely needs ______________ more!

3 He finds it weird ______________ so many cars in the parking lot. 11th grade students usually stop ______________ the school bus and start ______________ their own cars.

4 His classmates wanted him ______________ the math club because he's good with numbers, but he's decided ______________ sport.

b Write a blogpost about your experiences at school (200 words). Include details about your typical day, the subjects you study or extra activities you do. Use the verbs from the box followed by a gerund or *to*-infinitive.

advise ■ can't stand ■ decide ■ enjoy ■ hate ■ forget ■ remember ■ stop ■ want

____

____

____

____

____

____

____

20 High school in Finland and the USA

a Rasmus is writing a blog about his experiences in the USA. Put the words in the correct order to make sentences. Be careful – there are always some words you don't need.

1 knowing | to go | I am enjoying | if | to know | Friends at home | in Charleston | to school | want | going
2 I have decided | drama | as an elective | to take up | this year | taking up
3 putting on | at the end | I am looking forward | put on | a play | to | of the year
4 to drama school | to go | go back | I hope | I | going | to | when | to Finland

15 **b** Lindy, a reporter for her school's news website, interviews Rasmus. Listen to the interview and list the similarities and differences between the American and Finnish school systems and the German system.

USA	Finland	Germany

21 Same language?

16 **a** In the UK and the US, people speak English, but is it the same English? Listen to a teacher explaining the differences and do the tasks.

1 Explain why America and Britain are 'two nations divided by a common language'.
2 Identify the most noticeable difference between American and British English.
3 Complete the table with the missing words.

British English	American English
	gasoline
bonnet	
go to the toilet / loo	
	sweater
trainers	
	crosswalk

17 **b** Listen to some examples of British English and American English and write BE or AE next to each.

1 It's four kilometres away so I have to go by bike. ________
2 Dinner will be roast chicken, carrots, potatoes and turnips with tomato salad. ________
3 No matter what you say, say it in English! ________
4 Could you pass the salt, please? ________
5 That's all. I gotta go now. ________

17 **c** Listen again and try to pronounce the sentences like the speakers.

→ students' book, pages 58/59

Practice: The school year

22 **An Irish guide to American high schools.** Conor promised to write blogposts for his class blog back in Ireland. Read his latest article and complete it with the correct form of the verbs in brackets.

Most Irish students only know about American high school customs from Hollywood films and sitcoms. This article also looks at some facts about everyday life in American high schools, which those of you who are considering ________________ (1) (*spend*) some time here might want ________________ (2) (*know*) about.

I really enjoy ________________ (3) (*watch*) is a high school marching band. These bands are huge armies of students playing different instruments who perform at events during the school year. Many bands also perform at state level and they are expected ____________________ (4) (*take part*) in competitions. The very best are invited ____________________________ (5) (*compete*) at what Americans call 'nationals'.

Bands of America (BOA) hosts regional championships for high school marching bands in the United States, including the annual BOA Grand National Championships. By founding, Marching Bands of America in 1975, Larry McCormick hoped ____________________ (6) (*provide*) educational opportunities for music students. If a student wants to join the school marching band, MBA recommends ____________________ (7) (*apply*) for a scholarship which can help them ____________________ (8) (*reduce*) what they pay in tuition.

High school marching bands perform at different events during the year, so they need to have a suitable venue. Generally, things are really big in the US, but I can't help ________________ (9) (*be*) impressed by the size of auditoriums and gymnasiums at the average American high school. I can't imagine ________________ (10) (*find*) such a big gym at an Irish school! They host basketball matches and marching band performances as well as cheerleading. Cheerleading is considered ________________ (11) (*be*) an iconic American activity symbolizing school spirit, leadership and youthfulness. It is an important part of sporting events. Thanks to American movies and TV, it has become popular around the world. If you'd like ________________ (12) (*become*) a cheerleader, you need to have good coordination and basic dance skills, be able to memorize complicated choreography and show complete dedication.

23 College in the US

a Cara, Conor's Irish school friend, would like to attend college in the US. She has written an email to him asking for advice. Circle the correct words to complete the sentences she says.

Hi Conor,

Sorry I forgot **to answer / answering** (1) your last email, but I've been really busy at school, with exams and projects … Well, you know what it's like! Anyway, how are things up there? I'm sure you're having a great time and I hope the weather's better than it is here!
You know I've always enjoyed **to study /studying** (2) Biology, so I've decided **to go / going** (3) to university to study Biomedical Science. I looked for information and it seems there are some very good universities in South Carolina. My parents would like me **to study / studying** (4) there, too! Of course, they expect me **to get / getting** (5) a holiday job to help **to pay / paying** (6) for everything. But I don't mind **to do / doing** (7) that if I can come! Mum and Dad have some good friends living on Myrtle Beach and they would love **to have / having** (8) me around. I remember **to spend / spending** (9) the holidays there three years ago. We all fell in love with the place. It's so different from Dublin!
So, I thought it would be a perfect place to go. I also thought that, as you've been living there for some time now, you might be able to give me some advice.
Of course, I plan **to look up / looking up** (10) information on the internet about universities, places to live and all that, but **to have / having** (11) your advice would be much better! OK, I must stop **to write / writing** (12) and get back to my last school project.

Lots of love,
Cara

b Here are the notes Conor has made for Cara. Write Conor's reply giving information, using the expressions and verbs from the box.

You should try … ■ You'd better … ■ If I were you … ■ allow ■ ask ■ choose ■ expect ■ forget ■ like ■ need ■ want

- four very good unis in South Carolina – check websites for details
- apply in advance online / allow plenty of time – takes months
- pass the ACT (American College Testing) (core subjects: Math, English, Science)
- strong scholarship programmes – check: reduces tuition costs
- accommodation: college apartments, student house or rent a flat – too expensive (have to cook, clean, … ☹)
- campus: lots of people, make friends easily, meals cooked for you, cleaning service, fun!
- get student visa – after place at college confirmed
- details: contact international admissions office

24 WRITING FOCUS: School and education in Germany

a You have been asked to write a blogpost about school and education in Germany for foreign students wanting to come on exchange programmes. Decide what aspects of the topic you are going to focus on, e.g. age, legal requirements, academic requirements, scholarships, regional differences, etc.

b Brainstorm ideas in note form. Write as many as you wish. You can select the most relevant later.

c Select the ideas you will use.

d Structure your blogpost. Decide what information you are going to include in each section and how many paragraphs you are going to write.

- Introduction
- Middle paragraphs
- Conclusion

e Write your blogpost (about 150 to 200 words).

Weekend in the city

25 Conor's home city

18 **a** Conor is telling Meg about Dublin, his home city. Listen to their conversation and tick (✓) the topics they talk about.

☐ Architecture	☐ Government	☐ Population	☐ Food
☐ History	☐ Monuments	☐ Cultural events	☐ Night life

18 **b** Listen again and decide if these sentences are true (T) or false (F). Correct the false ones.

		T	F
1	The Vikings settled in Dublin in the 9th century.	☐	☐
2	The Normans invaded Ireland from France.	☐	☐
3	You can travel from France to Ireland in less than five hours by sea.	☐	☐
4	The Brazen Head is Dublin's oldest pub.	☐	☐
5	Temple Bar is the cultural heart of the city.	☐	☐
6	Dublin has approximately the same size population as Charleston.	☐	☐

c Complete these questions Meg asks Conor using question tags.

1 You're from Dublin, ____________________?

2 They were in France, ____________________?

3 They didn't sail all the way up to Ireland, ____________________?

4 It's quite an old city, ____________________?

5 I could talk to my parents and we could go this summer, ____________________?

6 That would be fantastic, ____________________?

26 **A conversation.** Meg is talking to her parents. Listen and answer the questions.

19

1 What are they talking about?

____.

2 What does 'smell a rat' mean?

____.

3 Why is Meg's so interested in going to Dublin?

____.

4 What does Meg's father mean when he says, 'father's intuition'?

____.

27 Planning a holiday

a Meg and her parents are planning the summer holidays. Rewrite the questions.

1 Have you booked the tickets?

I was wondering ______________________________.

2 What time is the flight?

Do you know ______________________________?

3 How do we get from the airport to the city centre?

I'm not sure ______________________________.

4 Should we take a raincoat or a light jacket?

I can't decide ______________________________.

b Meg and Conor are looking at a tourist's guide to Dublin. Complete what Conor says.

- You can't miss Dublin Castle, St Patrick's Cathedral and Christ Church Cathedral!
- Sightseeing on a hop-on-hop-off bus at the cheapest prices!
- Have a picnic in Phoenix Park and spend a relaxing afternoon at Dublin Zoo or visiting the Wellington Monument.
- If you love books and architecture, you must visit Trinity College Library, one of the most beautiful libraries in the world!
- One of the best day trips out of the city – and a must-see during your trip to Dublin – is a tour of Wicklow Mountains.

Meg: My mom would like to visit some interesting sights? What do you think?

Conor: The most interesting ______________________________. (1)

Meg: What about sightseeing? What do you suggest?

Conor: The cheapest way ______________________________. (2)

Meg: Are there any quiet parks where we can have a picnic?

Conor: Yes, sure. ______________________________. (3)

Meg: Are there any nice libraries?

Conor: Of course! ______________________________. (4)

Meg: My parents like hiking a lot. What would you recommend?

Conor: The best place ______________________________. (5)

Practice: City and country

28 Life in the country

a Nick has lived in the countryside and in big cities. Jada has only lived in a big city. Read what Nick says and complete the text with words from the boxes.

find ■ have (2x) ■ pick ■ swim ■ walk ■ watch	what ■ where ■ whether ■ who

I've lived in many different places. I was born and raised in the countryside and, ______________ (1) experienced city life as a teenager, I think I have had the best and worst of both worlds. I grew up in a cottage just a few metres from the beach, a few kilometres from the nearest town. My brothers and I spent much of our time outside, ______________ (2) in the sea in the summer, ______________ (3) along the cliffs, ______________ (4) berries and ______________ (5) the dolphins from our front garden. I had no idea ______________ (6) living in a city was like. Everyone in the village knew ______________ (7) we were and we knew everyone. We knew ______________ (8) ______________ (9) our parents – at Emma's café. It was the best place ______________ (10) hot chocolate in winter and lemonade in summer. However, I'm not sure ______________ (11) I want that kind of life now that I'm 15 because there are disadvantages, too.

b Jada is asking Nick about his life in the countryside. Complete her part of the conversation.

1 Let's talk about ____________________ your everyday life was like.
2 I was wondering ____________________ you managed without an internet connection.
3 Can you tell me ____________________ you went with your friends at weekends?
4 I'm wondering ____________________ I'd want to live in a place like that.

20 **c** Jada is now speaking about her life in a big city. Listen and complete the sentences.

1 Jada doesn't know ____.
2 She understands ____.
3 In a big city, she has to tell her parents ______________________________.
4 She can go to shops ____.
5 She doesn't worry ____.
6 She really doesn't know ____.

»» **d** What are the pros and cons of living in a big city or in the countryside? Consider what Nick and Jada said and your own experiences and write about 200 words.

29 Too many tourists?

a Read this article about tourism. Find words in the text that match the definitions.

1 a situation in which someone moves into a different social class ____________________

2 methods that do not harm the environment ____________________

3 a lack of something that you need or want ____________________

4 money that someone gets from working or investments ____________________

5 having an effect or influence ____________________

6 included in something else, e.g. a system ____________________

In 2019, cruise ships unloaded 20 000 visitors each day in Barcelona, Venice was visited by 30 million people and 6 million tourists were attracted to the Grand Canyon in the USA.

On the positive side, tourists spend money and bring wealth to these areas. But they also bring pollution and cause problems with safety and accommodation. Whole apartment blocks have been converted to tourist accommodation, making it difficult for residents to rent or buy them. Although jobs are created for local people, they are typically low paid with limited opportunities for upward mobility.

So can tourism be sustainable? Many would argue that this is not possible. Negative effects such as water and energy shortages, greenhouse gas emissions and vast amounts of waste are difficult to avoid. According to the World Tourism Organization, sustainable tourism takes into account current and future economic, social and environmental impacts of tourism, while at the same time, addressing the needs of visitors, the environment and communities. It involves contributing to the economy by creating jobs and income, and helping to conserve local culture and identity.

But how can tourists help to make their presence less impactful? Some destinations have become too popular, but you can lower your impact by visiting at off-peak times or exploring some of their lesser-known sites. Try to use local businesses and rent accommodation directly from locals. Sustainability is also about being aware of the impact we have on a destination's culture. Be sensitive to cultural differences, find out about the local culture and show respect for traditions.

Hopefully, there will be a day when sustainability is built into every touristic business, but until then, we need to make our own small but important contribution.

b Summarize the main ideas of the article in your own words.

____

____

____

»» **c** Do you think tourism can be made sustainable? Why or why not? What can we do to make it more sustainable? Write about 200 words.

→ students' book, pages 62/63

30 READING FOCUS: Illinois

a Read the article and give it a title. Then write a heading for each paragraph.

(TITLE) ______________________________

(1) ______________________________

There is a lot of debate in the US about the country's urban-rural divide. Rural areas are poorer than urban ones. People with a college education move to urban places because they offer better opportunities. Globalization and technological change help urban areas and drain human and material resources from the heartland, frequently depriving it of opportunity. This is the case in Illinois.

(2) ______________________________

When people think of Illinois, they generally think of Chicago. However, Illinois is a surprisingly complex state, with diverse geography and socio-economic conditions. Statistics show that the population has grown slowly over the last 20 years, but most of this growth has occurred in urban counties. Many young people have moved to towns and cities, so the average age of the population in rural areas is increasing. This puts more pressure on the healthcare system.

(3) ______________________________

When people in urban areas think about rural places, they mistakenly assume that agriculture is the main sector. In the past, farm implement and appliance manufacturers had large facilities in rural Illinois. Manufacturing jobs remain significant and there has been some growth, e.g. food processing plants and the manufacturing of building materials. However, many manufacturing jobs have been outsourced or made redundant through the introduction of technology.

(4) ______________________________

The use of technology on farms increases work rate, but it has caused a decline in the importance of agricultural employment because it reduces the number of farms and farm workers. This also has a negative impact on the population. As the farm population decreases, there is less demand for shops, health care and education in these areas.

b Find words in the article that match these definitions and highlight them.

1 to use so much of something that you make somewhere weaker or poorer
2 the central part of a country
3 to purchase products or goods from an outside company
4 when someone is told they must leave their job because they are no longer needed

c Write definitions for two more words or expressions in the article. Swap what you have written with a partner and find your partner's expressions in the article.

____

____

____

How to collect and present survey results

31 Collecting and presenting information. Conor's school carried out a survey amongst 1000 students to find out their preferred career choices. Multiple answers were possible. Look at the bar chart and write a report. Use the bar chart and expressions from the box.

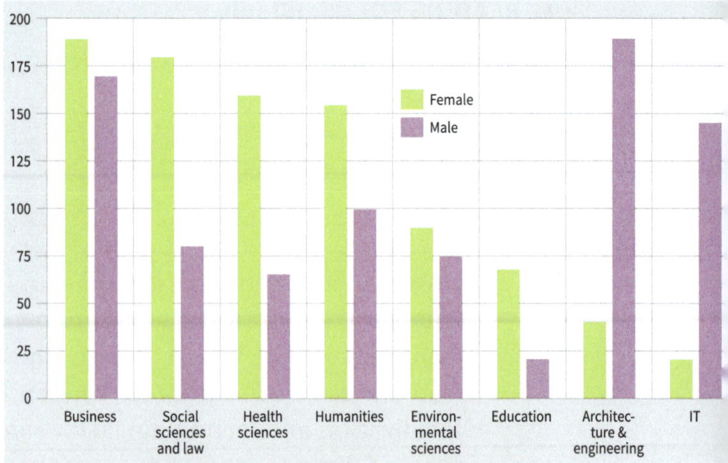

- We conducted a survey about … / carried out a survey to find out …
- The number of … interviewed was …
- 1000 students were asked about … / asked to choose … / asked to fill in the questionnaire about …
- There were … (questions, categories, etc.) in the survey.
- The result shows that …
- The majority / Most of the interviewees …
- More than / Less than … of the interviewees …
- The most / least popular … was … / … was chosen by / was selected by …
- … was chosen by the highest / lowest number of …
- In conclusion, it can be (clearly) seen that the survey shows that …

32 Presenting your results. On page 43, you conducted a survey to find out how interested in music students in your school are. Choose the best way to present your results: a pie chart or a bar chart. Give reasons for your decision. Create your chart with the results. Prepare your survey report. Decide how to organize the information. Then write your report (about 200 words) explaining the information you collected. You can use expressions from the box.

33 Creating a presentation. Prepare a presentation to show how you conducted your survey and got your results. Use expressions from the box. Then present the results of your survey to the class.

Mediation

34 Brooklyn Free School

a You have chosen to spend a year at Brooklyn Free School. Write a blogpost in German about the school and your plans. Tell your readers why this school is different from other schools, what is taught there, how students learn, and how problems among students are solved at this school.

What We Do

EQUAL PARTNERS

There is no one way to learn at Brooklyn Free School. Our students are challenged and supported by a community of self-directed learning. At BFS we have no standardized curriculum, no mandatory testing, and no grading. Our teachers work with students to develop a curriculum that supports their passions and their growth, and our lessons leap out of the classroom and into our neighborhood, city, and wider world. Our curriculum fosters self-confidence and self-motivation, as students learn that they are equal partners in determining their educational paths.

THE SCHOOL AS A COMMUNITY

[...] Through our system of democratic meetings, [...] students solve individual and community problems through discussion, debate, and cooperation, and contribute to the running of the school as a whole. This is in the context of a school population whose diversity – in terms of race, income, ability, and background – is rare in New York City, and rarer still in the broader United States.

GROWING AT BFS

At Brooklyn Free School we believe in the potential of education to transform ourselves at the deepest levels of who we are, and we know that this kind of learning means embracing play, curiosity, and, yes, discomfort, too. A BFS student leaves the school with a complex and comprehensive education, and the personal integrity and courage to continue a life of exploration and questioning.

HIGH SCHOOL PROGRAM

We know teens are energetic, curious, and ready to engage meaningfully with their world. We embrace these gifts as we guide, challenge, and support our high school students in the creation of a personalized education. Students fulfill (and exceed) New York State High School requirements with a mix of structured, staff-led classes, projects, and activities, independent studies, in-school leadership and responsibilities, and citywide internships, volunteering, and student programs.
Our high school kindles a love of learning, and enhances the capacity for disciplined study – necessary, and much sought, attributes for success in college and along any other path students choose to follow. [...]

www.brooklynfreeschool.org

b Your mother thinks that Brooklyn Free School could be a good option for you. But she has some questions. You contact the school and ask questions. Write an email.

Könntest du vielleicht die Schule anschreiben, um ein paar Dinge zu klären? Ich wüsste gern, ob es etwas kostet, wenn du dahin gehst. Frag auch mal nach, ob sie überhaupt deutsche Gastschülerinnen und Gastschüler aufnehmen und wie die Anmelderegularien sind. Vielleicht ist es möglich, dass du in der Schule wohnen kannst. Oder hat die Schule Kontaktdaten von Familien, die in der Nähe wohnen und Gastschülerinnen und Gastschüler aufnehmen? Frage da bitte auch nach und stelle am besten auch gleich noch die Fragen, die dir in den Sinn kommen. Ich bin mir sicher, du möchtest auch noch ein paar Dinge wissen.

My review

1 About relationships
1 've been
2 for
3 have been playing
4 have made
5 have not spoken
6 yet
7 's been playing
8 've been hoping
9 've met
10 since

2 About fashion
1 online
2 thrift
3 second-hand
4 look
5 bargain
6 'll give
7 trends
8 had
9 allowance
10 fast
11 exploited
12 label
13 in-store
14 don't know
15 thought

3 About city and country life
1 Hectic
2 laid-back
3 peaceful
4 noisy
5 dangerous
6 cultural
7 interesting
8 diverse
9 friendly
10 rural

4 About school systems
1 to do
2 to talk
3 to get lost
4 feeling
5 to ask
6 to spend
7 joining
8 going
9 thinking
10 to get to know
11 wearing
12 to buy
13 seeing
14 to focus
15 coming

Modern technology

1 Then and now

a Complete the sentences about how everyday activities were done in the past and are done now. Use the passive in the simple present, simple past or present perfect.

1 **In the past:** Any dust on the floor at home ______________ (1) (*sweep up*) with a broom or a brush. The dust ______________ (2) (*collect*) in a dustpan. Then it ______________ (3) (*take*) outside and ______________ (4) (*empty*) into a rubbish bin.
Now: Our lives ______________ (5) (*transform*) by the vacuum cleaner. The machine ______________ (6) (*plug*) into the nearest power socket and ______________ (7) (*turn on*). The machine ______________ (8) (*move*) over the carpet by the person doing the cleaning and all the dust ______________ (9) (*suck up*).

2 **In the past:** Any items you wanted to buy ______________ (10) (*pay for*) in cash in stores. Some items ______________ (11) (*order*) from mail order catalogues and cheques ______________ (12) (*use*) to pay for them.
Now: Purchases ______________ (13) (*make*) with cash, a bank card, a credit card or even with your smartphone. Payment apps ______________ (14) (*download*) by many people from app stores to their phones nowadays. Your phone ______________ (15) (*scan*) by a machine and the money ______________ (16) (*take out*) of your account.

b Think of another everyday activity which is different today than it was in the past because of technology. Use the correct form of the passive and write a short text (about 100 words) about how things were done in the past and are done now.

2 **A time capsule.** A time capsule is a box into which people put information or objects that show what life is like today. You bury it and hope that people in the future will find it and learn about life in the past. Work with a partner and and write a text for your time capsule.

1 What technology do you use in your everyday life?
2 How do you usually travel?
3 Describe the activities that you do in your free time and explain what role technology plays in these activities.

3 Photography: Past, present and future

a Scan the texts (A – C) and label them past, present or future.

A ______________

Most photographs ______________________________ (1) smartphones or tablets, rather than a camera. The lens of the device's camera ______________________ (2) on the object or person that is going to be photographed. Then light enters the lens and the image is captured by a sensor and recorded by the camera's hardware. Photographs ______________________ (3) social media sites and websites in a matter of seconds. A new type of photo ______________________ ______________________________ (4) smartphone photography: the selfie. Because smartphones are so light, they can easily be used to take pictures of the photographer.

B ______________

We know that virtual reality (VR) and 3D images are increasing in popularity and it ______________________ ______________ (5) that photographers will want their photos to reflect these trends. The latest technology ____ (6) to create 3D models of their photographs, which means they can spin, zoom and move an object around in a picture. Looking at photographs ____ (7) a completely new experience if they're viewed through a VR headset. You may even be able to touch the objects. At the moment, the processes required to create such images take a lot of time, but that will improve in the future.

C ______________

The first camera was the pinhole camera which ______________________________ (8) an Arab physicist called Ibn al-Haytham (965-1040). In 16th-century Britain, it ______________________________ (9) the chemical silver chloride darkens and produces an image when exposed to light. Photography as we know it today, began in the 1830s in France when Joseph Nicéphore Niépce used a light box and chemicals to create an image on a metal plate. Similar experiments were done, but it wasn't until the 1880s that a flexible roll film was created by the Kodak company. Up to 100 photos ______________________________ (10).

b Read the texts again and complete them with the phrases from the box.

are taken ■ can be saved and uploaded to ■ could be taken and saved ■ could even be turned into ■ has already been used ■ has even been created by ■ is focused ■ can be expected ■ was discovered ■ was developed by

c Choose another thing that is different now. Do some research to find out how it was done in the past, how it is done now and predict how you think it will be done in the future.

____

____

Practice: Technology – good or bad?

4 Survivalists in the USA

a The author Tara Westover comes from a family of 'survivalists' in the USA. Choose the sentence which best describes what it means to be a 'survivalist'.
A 'survivalist' is someone, who …

1 lives in a rural community and uses plants and herbs to treat medical conditions.
2 prepares for possible future disasters but doesn't take part in mainstream society.
3 campaigns to disrupt the social and political order, locally and internationally.

Tara Westover was born in the rural community of Clifton, Idaho. She was the youngest of seven children and her parents were survivalists. They lived in fear of disruption to the social or political order, both in their town and the world, and isolated themselves from others. They were suspicious of doctors, hospitals, public schools and the federal government. Tara was born at home, never visited a doctor and was homeschooled. However, she has some happy memories of her unusual upbringing. She enjoyed taking long walks in the hills and riding horses with her brother Shawn.
The only children she knew were those from other survivalist families. One of her brothers taught her to read, and she studied the writings of 'The Church of Jesus Christ of Latter-day Saints' because her family were Mormons. But she never went to a formal lesson, and there were only a few textbooks in the house which she could use to teach herself. Tara decided that she wanted a formal education. She used her pocket money to buy textbooks and studied on her own to be able to go to college. She struggled to adjust to academic life and mainstream society at first, but she graduated with honours in 2008. She gained a Master's degree and PhD from the University of Cambridge and, in 2019, she became known to a larger public when her book *Educated* was published. Former President Barack Obama described the book, which details Tara's childhood, as 'remarkable'.

b Read the article to check your answer to **a**, then choose the summary with all the correct facts.

1 Tara had a difficult childhood and grew up without being able to read and write. Even though she hadn't passed any exams, she was allowed to study at universities in the US and the UK and went on to work for President Obama.
2 Tara had a happy childhood which allowed her to connect with nature. She was an enthusiastic member of the Mormon Church and received help from the church to attend university and publish a book about her faith.
3 Tara had an unusual childhood and no formal education until she started college. She went on to achieve academic success and write a popular book about her experiences.

c Read again. Are the sentences true (T), false (F) or not in the text (N)?
Correct the false sentences.

	T	F	N
1 Tara was an only child who grew up in rural Idaho.	☐	☐	☐
2 Tara has happy childhood memories of being outdoors with her family.	☐	☐	☐
3 Tara grew up in a household where there were no textbooks to read.	☐	☐	☐
4 Tara met President Obama when her book was published.	☐	☐	☐

d Find words or phrases in the text that match these definitions.

1 a break or an interruption in normal life or events ______________________

2 a long way away from other people and communities ______________________

3 to have a serious distrust of something or someone ______________________

5 **An interview.** You're interviewing an expert on the Internet of Things. Complete the interview with the correct passive form of the verbs in brackets.

You So the Internet of Things, or 'IoT', is something that ______________________ (1) (*talk*) about for a quite a long time now. People are saying that the way we communicate with each other ______________________ (2) (*change*) completely by this new innovation when it is available. Today, we don't seem to be any closer to having the Internet of Things in our homes, schools or workplaces, but I hope that the Internet of Things ______________________ (3) (*can explain*) by the expert I'm interviewing today. She is a scientist at a local university where more tests ______________________ (4) (*do*) next month using the Internet of Things. So could you start, please, by telling us what the Internet of Things is?

Expert Of course. This is a term which ______________________ (5) (*use*) to describe a wide range of different systems where objects ______________________ (6) (*can control*) by the internet. Even if you don't realize it, you're already using the Internet of Things if, for example, you have a home where the lights and the thermostat ______________________ (7) (*turn on*) by an app or a computer system.

You So a lot of us are already using this innovative technology, but we don't know it?

Expert Yes, that's right. We could even say that smartphones are a part of a system we can call the Internet of Things. Some people don't take this very seriously as a concept. I think this is because, so far it ______________________ (8) (*present*) as a hi-tech way of controlling objects and allowing them to 'talk' to each other. That hasn't happened yet and we're not sure when that kind of technology ______________________ (9) (*adopt*) by normal people like you and me. More importantly, we aren't sure how useful that will really be at the moment either. But, if we think about all the progress which ______________________ (10) (*make*) in the last 20 – 30 years, it is clear that we have a lot to look forward to in the future!

→ students' book, pages 80/81

6 WRITING FOCUS: Pros and cons of homeschooling

a Katie, whose family lives off the grid in England, is being interviewed for a podcast about homeschooling. Before you listen, make notes about the pros and cons of being homeschooled.

21 **b** Listen to the interview and tick (✓) the pros and cons from your table in **a** that Katie mentions. Add more pros and cons she mentions in the table.

Pros	Cons

c Read the summary of the interview. Use different colours and mark the parts where the writer …
- mentions the exact words used in the interview.
- gives wrong or inaccurate information.
- adds information that wasn't in the interview.
- uses their own words to describe information.

> Katie is one of a large number of children in the UK who are homeschooled. Homeschooling has become more popular recently because children are only taught a narrow range of subjects at school. You can also choose exactly which subjects you want to study and how much time you spend on each subject. Katie likes the fact that she can study when she wants, although she might find it harder to get used to the working day when she's older if she doesn't learn to work to a specific schedule. Katie sometimes misses spending time with people her own age and finds it harder to take part in activities like sports. She also worries that homeschooling may not be a good preparation for university.

d Read the sentences from the interview and write a shorter sentence to paraphrase them.

1 I heard that 0.5 per cent of children are homeschooled here, which is a tiny amount, but the numbers have increased by about 40 per cent over the last few years and I imagine it'll become even more popular in the future.

____

____.

2 You can have live online lessons for any subject with teachers from all over the world. You can learn French from a French teacher in France, for example, or Maths from a Maths expert in the USA.

____

____.

3 I sometimes find it difficult to get up early and start learning early in the morning, but because I'm homeschooled it isn't a problem if I don't start my lessons until 10 o'clock – I just carry on studying later in the afternoon than school pupils do.

____

____.

Inventions and innovations

7 **Mike's idea.** Read the conversation between Ellie and her friend Mike about ideas for new inventions and innovations. Complete the conversation using a word from the same family as the words in brackets.

Mike Ellie, have I ever told you about my idea for an ____________________ (1) (*innovation*) way of ordering food from restaurants to eat at home?

Ellie I don't think so. What is it and how would it work?

Mike Well, it's simple really. I'm developing an app which you can download. It shows you the menus of all the restaurants in your area that have agreed to take part. Then you choose the food you want to order from one of those restaurants, and someone delivers it to you. I only have a ____________________ (2) (*prototypical*) at the moment, but I'm going to do some more work on it soon. What do you think?

Ellie Well, I think you want to ____________________ (3) (*avoidable*) making your app too similar to other food delivery apps out there. You aren't the first person to ____________________ (4) (*invention*) an app like this.

Mike Yes, but it's so hard to think of a totally original business idea.

Ellie Why don't you take a look at the other apps? Do some thinking about how you could ____________________ (5) (*improvement*) them. Try to have a Eureka moment! Or perhaps you could develop an app to help people in poorer parts of the world? I was reading an article about delivery drivers in Kenya. They have to travel long distances and then they have to wait till they've been paid for the item they've delivered. Perhaps we could think of a ____________________ (6) (*solve*) to that problem.

Mike That sounds interesting. We could try to find some ____________________ (7) (*invest*) in the US who want to support the first phase of development.

Ellie Wait a second! We need a real idea before we start thinking about that!

Mike Perhaps we could work with the government of a country to ____________________ (8) (*promotion*) self-service parcel collection.

Ellie That could work if we had a ____________________ (9) (*connect*) to someone in the government. I'm not exactly sure how we'd do that. Let's brainstorm some ideas.

Mike Great! I think this could be a really good project. Let's start looking for some ____________________ (10) (*inform*) on the internet!

8 A young innovator

22 **a** Listen to Tamara talking about becoming an innovator. Are the sentences true (T) or false (F)? Correct the false sentences.

		T	F
1	Tamara came up with the idea for her invention after receiving Christmas presents that she didn't like.	☐	☐
2	Tamara took a way of doing something that other apps were already using and applied it to another situation.	☐	☐
3	Tamara's app will only give gift recommendations; it doesn't show users where they can buy the gifts.	☐	☐
4	Tamara had originally expected it to take just under a year to develop the first version of her app.	☐	☐
5	The first app developer she worked with left the project because things were moving too slowly.	☐	☐
6	Tamara invested her own money in the app development, without knowing if she would get her money back.	☐	☐

22 **b** Listen again and copy the table. Make notes on what helped Tamara to develop her app and what she would do differently next time. Then compare your notes with a partner.

Things that helped her	Things she would do differently

c Complete the sentences about how Tamara's app works. Use the words from the box.

choose ■ display ■ enter ■ press ■ provide

1 Information about your friends and family members' interests ______________________ ______________________ into the app by the user.

2 The button at the bottom of the screen ______________________ by the user.

3 The best present ideas for the person ______________________ by the app's algorithms.

4 The results ______________________ on the screen for the user to see.

5 Links to stores where users can buy the gifts ______________________.

Practice: The inventor's world

9 **Tamara's app: one year later.** A year ago, Tamara launched her app. Read part of a magazine article about young innovators and complete it with the correct words.

Young inventors

Tamara was 15 years old when her idea for a gift-finding app ______________ (1) (*born*). The name 'Gift It' ________________ (2) (*choose*) for obvious reasons and the app has really taken off! In fact, it is estimated that the app ________________ (3) (*use*) by over one million people next Christmas. Young people are particularly keen on it because gifts for their family members ________________ (4) (*can find*) at the tap of a button, but it __________________________ (5) (*already download*) by many older people, too. Since 'Gift It' ________________ (6) (*launch*) last year, the problem of finding gifts for people in your family ________________ (7) (*solve*). And it's so simple. Once a few questions __________________________ (8) (*answer*), the perfect present ________________ (9) (*calculate*) by the app's amazing algorithms. Tamara worked very hard on the app and a lot of her own money ________________ (10) (*invest*). Now it looks like all of that hard work and her investment have paid off! We look forward to seeing 'Gift It' go from strength to strength next year.

10 **A talk about an American inventor.** Put sentences A – F from a high school student's talk about an American inventor into the correct order (1 – 6).

☐ **A** In other words, Carrier succeeded in developing his most famous invention because he wasn't afraid to send his ideas to others and see what they thought of them.

☐ **B** This brings me to my next point: how Carrier came up with the idea for air conditioning. A company in New York was having an air quality problem and invited engineers to send in ideas to deal with it. Carrier made drawings for a system which could deal with the problem and then built it.

☐ **C** Hello everyone. I'd like to talk to you today about the American inventor, Willis Carrier. You may not know his name, but you all know his invention. It's air conditioning!

☐ **D** Finally, I want to say that Willis Carrier was a very innovative problem-solver who wasn't afraid to take risks in order to develop new technologies.

☐ **E** There are two main points I'd like to discuss. I'll start by giving some background information about Carrier. Then I'll talk about his invention.

☐ **F** First, let's go back to Carrier's early life. He was born in 1876 in Angola in the state of New York and he grew up there. In 1900, he graduated from Cornell University with a Bachelor of Engineering degree.

→ students' book, pages 84/85

11 **The human computer.** Choose the correct verb forms to complete the text about American space innovator Katherine Johnson.

Katherine Johnson **wasn't expected to see / didn't expect to be seen** (1) as an American hero. Nevertheless, she made a significant contribution to the American space programme. In 2015, she **is awarded / was awarded** (2) the Presidential Medal of Freedom, which is the highest non-military medal that **can be given / can given** (3) by the American president.

Katherine loved maths while growing up in the small town of White Sulphur Springs, West Virginia, in the 1920s and 1930s. Her talent for the subject **was recognized from / was recognized by** (4) her parents, who arranged for her to attend a high school on the campus of West Virginia State College. At the age of just fourteen, she **was accepted / is accepted** (5) by the college, which was open to African Americans like Johnson, in order to study maths. A career as a maths teacher and higher studies in maths **brought / were brought** (6) to an end when Johnson became a mother, but she was still determined to become a research mathematician.

In 1952, Johnson **told / was told** (7) about a job at NASA by a family member and decided to apply for it. She didn't think that she would be given particularly important work to do in her job as a 'human computer'. However, her ability to calculate key information for space missions quickly and without making any mistakes **was soon noticed / were soon noticed** (8) by many of the astronauts who regularly asked for her support.

Johnson became a role-model for other female and African-American mathematicians and her example **has used / has been used** (9) to inspire them to believe there are no limits to what they can achieve. Johnson was also happy to share her knowledge with other people and 26 of her academic papers were published during her lifetime. Although Johnson died in 2020, her work and memory lives on. In the year of her death, a satellite named 'Katherine' **has been launched / was launched** (10) into space by NASA in her memory.

12 **Some young inventors are talking about their experiences.** Rewrite the active sentences as passive sentences. Use the correct object or the passive infinitive.

1 The local government took some of these services away last year.

____

____.

2 The school has given young inventors financial support to help them develop their ideas.

____.

3 Joe showed our prototype to another group of investors yesterday.

____.

4 I hadn't expected them to give me a prize for my invention.

____.

13 LISTENING FOCUS: Four inventors

23 **a** Listen to the information about four inventors. Make some notes about each innovator. Listen again. What do they all have in common?

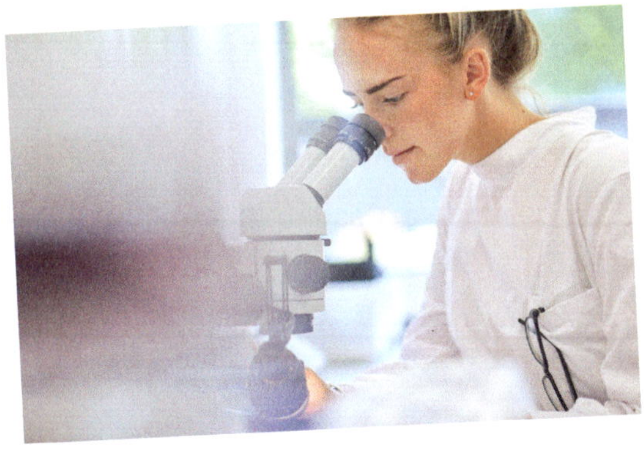

- ☐ 1 They were all born in the USA.
- ☐ 2 They are all younger than 20.
- ☐ 3 All of their inventions and innovations have something to do with the environment.
- ☐ 4 Everybody made a prototype of their product.

23 **b** Listen again and match the people to the things they invented.

Hannah
Rifath
Julian
Keiana

methods for detecting chemicals
an electricity generator
a device with sensors
a satellite

23 **c** Listen again and answer the questions. Which inventor …

1 invented something as a result of a childhood hobby? ______
2 has found a hi-tech way of identifying a problem? ______
3 was inspired to invent something by a major local event? ______
4 was given a prize for his / her invention? ______
5 was able to find a cheaper way of doing something? ______
6 used the latest technology to test his / her idea? ______

d Make notes on the characteristics that each inventor has. Use the words in the box to help you.

can keep going in spite of setbacks ■ creative ■ curious ■ innovative ■ problem-solver ■ self-motivated ■ takes risks ■ team player ■ very energetic

______
______
______
______
______

e With your partner, discuss which achievements you think are the most impressive and will have the greatest impact. Comment on what lessons you can learn from these teenage inventors.

Write a plan for your idea

14 ***Bike 2 U***

a Read the information about a business idea that some students have and do the tasks.

1 Outline what problems or challenges this idea solves.
2 Explain who will benefit from this idea.
3 Comment on who will pay for this service.

Our business idea is called Bike 2 U and it's a mobile bike repair service. If you have a bike which needs to be repaired, you go to our website or use our app, register with some personal information, for example, your address, and then tell us about the problem with your bike. We will then come to the place where you live – on our bikes, of course – and repair your bike for you. So you don't have to carry or drive your broken bike to a bike shop. The service will be available from early in the morning until the evening seven days a week, so customers are sure to find a time that suits them. Also, because we don't have to rent a place to do the repairs in, we can offer repairs at a lower price than bike shops.

b Read the three parts of the students' business plan and label them with the correct headings in the box.

Market ■ Problem ■ Solution

________________ Set up a mobile bike repairs service so that people can have their bikes repaired at home and don't have to transport them to a bike shop. Our service is also available for more hours than a bike shop would be open, so there is more flexibility for customers. The mechanics can also carry all of the equipment and parts they need with them while riding to the customer's home to repair their bike. The customers also pay less to have their bikes repaired than they would if they took them to a repair shop.

________________ This service would be suitable for all age groups and types of people who ride a bike. It would be particularly suitable for young people because they are more flexible during the day, so the bike mechanic could come to their address then.

________________ It can be difficult and inconvenient for people to bring their bikes to a bike repair shop. Repairs at a bike shop can be more expensive because the bike shop owners have to pay to rent the building and pay for electricity and other costs. You can also pay mechanics a lot less money if they're travelling to people's homes rather than working in a bike repair shop.

c Read the business plan again. Identify and write three possible problems with it.

1 ________________________

2 ________________________

3 ________________________

____

It's our planet, too!

15 A school action plan

a The Green Action Group is unhappy about the measures adopted last year and has written a report with their recommendations. Choose the correct verb forms to complete it.

School Action Plan

We, the Green Action Group, feel that our school is still not doing enough to protect the environment. We have outlined the main problems below and made some suggestions.

1 Too much unnecessary electricity is used. We **wouldn't have used / hadn't used** (1) so much electricity and **would have saved / had saved** (2) money last year if students and staff **wouldn't have remembered / had remembered** (3) to switch off all electrical equipment after each lesson.
Action point: Put up notices to remind people to switch off computers and lights when they leave a room.

2 Too many food leftovers are thrown away. If the canteen **would have taken up / had taken up** (4) our suggestion to buy a compost bin, we **could have done / had done** (5) something useful with leftover food.
Action point: Buy a compost bin and install it behind the kitchen.

3 Not enough items are recycled. We **would have recycled / had recycled** (6) a lot of waste last year if we **would have established / had established** (7) a clear recycling system, like the German system.
Action point: Introduce a recycling system with different-colored bins for different types of waste.

4 Too much single-use plastic is used. We **would have reduced / had reduced** (8) plastic waste if the canteen **wouldn't have continued / hadn't continued** (9) serving drinks in plastic bottles or with plastic straws.
Action point: We should ban plastic bottles and plastic straws. If the catering manager **would not have ignored / hadn't ignored** (10) our recommendations last year, as well as using less plastic, we **would have saved / had saved** (11) money, which **had been used / could have been used** (12) to implement further green measures.

b Complete these sentences with the verbs in brackets in the correct form.

1 If we ________________ (*discuss*) these problems more seriously last year, we ________________ (*find*) some solutions.
2 The committee members ________________ (*not speak*) the head teacher yesterday if they ________________ (*not think*) she could help them.
3 If we ________________ (*buy*) more recycling bins, we ________________ (*recycle*) 80% of the rubbish we threw away last year.
4 We ________________ (*start*) working on the action points a lot sooner if you ________________ (*email*) the plan to everyone more quickly.
5 If we ________________ (*ask*) the media to report on our campaign, we ________________ (*get*) some local people and companies interested in what we are trying to do.

16 **Plastic-free shopping.** Read the article about the growing popularity of stores without plastic packaging and complete it with the correct conjunctions from the box. You will need to use some of the conjunctions more than once.

after ■ as soon as ■ before ■ until ■ when

It will not be much longer ________________ (1) a new type of store becomes a normal sight in every German town. Plastic has been such an important part of the shopping experience ________________ (2) now. So ________________ (3) you think of a shop that sells food, you usually imagine lots of packaging and plastic containers.
However, as we see in plastic-free stores, it is possible to avoid using any plastic, but the store looks a little bit different than you would expect. ________________ (4) you walk into a plastic-free store, you notice all the containers on the walls from which customers can take different foods and other products. ________________ (5) you are shopping at a plastic-free store, you need to either use containers you have brought from home and fill them with products, or purchase recyclable containers from the store for a small deposit. ________________ (6) the customers have taken the amount of muesli, cheese or washing powder that they need, they pay for the exact amount in their containers. This results in a lot less food waste.
________________ (7) you go to a plastic-free store for the first time, you may wonder if it will take you longer to buy your groceries. But ________________ (8) you start filling up your plastic boxes, you'll find that the experience can actually be quite fun. People who use plastic-free stores usually enjoy the shopping experience and are glad to do something to help the environment, too. However, it may be some time ________________ (9) everyone starts shopping in this way.

→ students' book, pages 90/91

Practice: Saving the earth

17 **SPEAKING FOCUS: Giving a speech**

a Imagine you are an environmental campaigner. You are giving a speech to some politicians in order to convince them that they need to do more for the environment. Read part of your speech quietly. Make sure you know the right pronunciation and intonation for each word. Underline words you want to stress and mark where you want to pause.

For a long time now, scientists have been absolutely clear that action is needed to prevent a climate crisis on our planet. As we approach crisis point, politicians can no longer look away and claim that they're already doing as much as they can to help. The policies and solutions we currently have, are nowhere near good enough. You tell young people that you hear their voices and you know how urgent the situation is, but your actions don't convince me that you really mean what you say. This is difficult to accept because fully understanding the situation and failing to act is even worse than not understanding it and failing to act. How can our politicians – those who we elected to office – simply not care about the future of our country?

b Take turns to read your speech to a partner. Listen and give feedback on the following:

- how confidently your partner spoke.
- how easy it was to understand what your partner wanted to say.
- whether your partner paused at the appropriate points in the speech.
- whether your partner smiled and made eye contact with you.

c Based on your partner's feedback and the tips, make notes about what you could do to improve your public speaking.

d Practise your speech again and give each other feedback on whether you have improved in the areas you decided to focus on.

Public speaking tips

1 Relax! Pause, smile, and count to three before you say anything.
2 Speak clearly and confidently. Imagine that the audience is clapping – it will increase your confidence.
3 Pause after words you want the audience to remember.
4 Take your time! Speaking faster will make it hard for the audience to understand you.
5 Keep eye contact with the audience.

18 A meeting about the future of a music festival

a Three people who work for major charities involved in a big music festival in the UK are meeting with Louise, the festival's organizer, to discuss improvements to future festivals. Read part of the conversation from the meeting and do the tasks below.

Louise Thanks everyone for coming along today. As you know, the reason why we're here is to think of ideas to make our festival more inclusive and more environmentally friendly. Perhaps we could start with the first part. Would you like to say something about that, Roy? I know you focus on improving access for the disabled. Where could we improve?

Roy Well, could I just say thank you for the improvements you've made over the last few years, Louise. Up until then it seemed that you hadn't thought about the fact that disabled people might also want to join the festival ...

Louise That might be true, but I think that a lot of people were thinking that way, too, unfortunately – it wasn't just us.

Roy I'm not finished. I also wanted to say that we're grateful that you provided disabled toilets and ramps last year. That was great – we just need more of them next time.

Kristen I agree, Roy. It isn't enough to just say 'We have some facilities for the disabled'. You need to have good facilities for the disabled and enough of them.

Louise That's a good point. Let's increase the number of toilets and ramps next time.

Steve I'd just like to say that if we're talking about priorities here, reducing the amount of plastic used at the festival should be right at the top of the list.

Roy Sorry to interrupt here, but aren't people more important than plastic?

Steve You have a point, but if we don't protect our planet by reducing the amount of plastic we use – and waste – there'll be no planet left for people to live on in the future, Roy!

Louise I understand how you both feel. I think we can manage to provide better disabled access and reduce the amount of single-use plastic at the same time. Steve, maybe you can share some ideas for reducing single-use plastic with us ...

1 Outline two things that the speakers disagree on. ______________________

______________________.

2 Describe what they agree to do. ______________________

______________________.

3 Comment on whether you think the speakers disagree with and interrupt each other politely. How do you know? ______________________

______________________.

b Read the conversation again. Use different colours to highlight the phrases the speakers use to

1 agree 2 disagree 3 take turns

c Think of a regular event in your community. Think about how it could be made more inclusive and environmentally friendly. Come up with at least two suggestions for improvements.

19 Plogging

a What do you think the activity 'plogging' is about? Tick (✓) the answer you think is correct, then read the article. Where you correct?

- [ ] 1 Blogging about running with other people in public places.
- [ ] 2 Floating on logs down rivers with a group of strangers.
- [ ] 3 Running in a group while picking up all the litter you see.

'Plogging': A sport for the climate crisis generation?

Have you ever heard of 'plogging'? People have been doing it since 2016 and it may not have reached your part of the world yet. The word 'plogging' is an English word, but it is a combination of the word 'jogging' and the Swedish expression *plocka upp*, which means 'pick up'. As you might imagine 'plogging' combines running, or jogging, with picking up litter.

'Plogging' began in the Swedish capital Stockholm and has since spread to other countries. The picking up of litter while moving around your town or city can be a hard workout, which is good for the environment as well. You bend over to get the litter, pick it up and then stretch yourself out as you get back up again and start running, hiking or walking.

Erik Ahlström was the first 'plogger' and he created a website called *Plogga* to encourage volunteers to organize the runs and the recycling of waste the 'ploggers' collect. Due to Ahlström's efforts, several high profile individuals around the world have begun 'plogging', from the Indian Prime Minister Narendra Modi to the American author David Sedaris. Moreover, a US organization called *Keep America Beautiful* now promotes 'plogging' throughout the country.

We'll have to wait and see whether 'plogging' takes off and becomes an everyday activity in the same way that Nordic walking has. On the one hand, it doesn't seem to be a particularly exciting activity. On the other hand, it combines several key elements which are important to millennials and Generation Z: movement, community and helping the environment.

b Tell your partner what you think about 'plogging'. Would you like to do it? Explain why or why not.

c Do some research into one of these unusual activities and make notes.

1 Toy voyaging 2 Dog surfing 3 Extreme ironing

d Prepare a presentation on the activity you chose.

- Explain what the activity involves.
- Outline its history and development and how popular it is today.
- Explain why people do it and comment on whether it will be popular in the future.

Space adventures

20 An interview with an astronaut

24 **a** Listen to a student interviewing an astronaut. Tick (✓) the topics that he asks her questions about.

☐ 1 How you train to become an astronaut.
☐ 2 What personal qualities you need to become an astronaut.
☐ 3 What can go wrong when you're in space.
☐ 4 How astronauts eat and drink when they're in space.
☐ 5 How astronauts sleep when they're in space.
☐ 6 What the most enjoyable thing is about being in space.

24 **b** Listen again. Tick (✓) the interviewer's reaction to the astronaut's statements.

1 *You need to have a laugh and not take it all too seriously when things go wrong – because they will!* ☐ **a** very interested ☐ **b** very surprised

2 *We couldn't drink anything until the liquid melted.*
☐ **a** very worried ☐ **b** very frightened

3 *Sometimes you can feel yourself rotate as you're trying to get to sleep, which is actually quite a pleasant feeling!* ☐ **a** very jealous ☐ **b** very interested

c Complete the sentences with words you heard in the interview.

1 Astronauts need to be ______________________ because they will have to change the way they live to fit the situation they are in.

2 Astronauts have to be ______________________ because they often need ______________________.

3 Astronauts need to ______________________ their frozen food by adding water and then they can eat it.

4 When astronauts are ______________________, they don't need to walk anywhere. They can just move and float around wherever they want.

5 Astronauts sometimes move around in circles, or ______________________, while they're weightless in the space station.

6 Because there's so little gravity in space, astronauts just ______________________ up and down and round the space station or spaceship.

>>> **d** Think of three other questions for the astronaut. Then do some research to find the answers.

1 ____?
2 ____?
3 ____?

21 Making predictions

a Read the information about what is happening in the world today and write the predictions. Use the future perfect when you write your predictions.

1 The Amur leopard is one of the world's most endangered species of big cat. Amur leopards live in south-eastern Russia and northern China and, in recent years, their numbers have been decreasing significantly every year. There are estimated to be fewer than seventy of them living there today. These beautiful animals are at risk from hunters who want their fur or to use parts of their body in Chinese medicine. Logging and forest fires in their home regions also put Amur leopards at risk.

By 2040, Amur leopards ______________________________

______________________________.

2 Diesel car emissions are harmful for the environment and people's health. These emissions increase the risk of breathing problems and serious disease. Since the 1990s, the European Union has introduced more laws to stop people from driving them. Sales have fallen in busy cities such as Paris, Madrid and Hamburg, and some cities have even introduced zones where you cannot drive diesel cars. Today, many people are choosing to buy electric cars instead. Over the next decade, it is likely that most European cities will stop diesel cars from being bought or used at all.

By 2030, diesel cars ______________________________

______________________________.

3 Alzheimer's disease is a type of dementia. It causes people's brain tissue to break down and that makes it harder for them to remember things. Three different drugs are currently available which can slow down the damage to the brain and help to slow down the process of memory loss. Researchers are currently working hard to develop a cure for Alzheimer's as quickly as possible and they are optimistic that there will be more effective drugs, or even a cure, in the near future.

Before the end of this decade, researchers ______________________________

______________________________.

b Choose a topic and write your own prediction about it.

the importance of learning Mandarin ■ finding a cure for cancer ■ the giant panda ■ what clothes we will wear ■ what school will be like

____

____

____

→ students' book, pages 94/95

Practice: Life on Mars

22 **How sci-fi inspired science.** Complete the text with the future perfect form of the verbs.

You may be surprised to hear that a lot of the technologies we use today were first imagined by science-fiction writers long before their invention. The French author Jules Verne may have predicted more future technological developments than any other writer. He wrote this in the 19th century. 'In a few years' time people ____________________ (1) (*start*) building submarines and they ______________________________ (2) (*invent*) a 'phonotelephote' – a device that will let you see people when you talk to them on the phone.' Most of you probably know the TV show *Big Brother*, but you probably _________________________ (3) (*not read*) the novel *1984* by George Orwell, in which he writes that nobody will be able to keep anything secret any longer because 'Big Brother is watching' everyone all the time. He suggests that by 1984, governments ___________________________________ (4) (*decide*) to use video cameras – or 'telescreens'– to keep people under constant observation. Today, video cameras are common in many parts of the world.

A popular 1960s TV series called *Star Trek* inspired Martin Cooper at Motorola to start work on a device that changed communication forever. And his idea? That by the 22nd century, people _________________________________ (5) (*develop*) devices called 'communicators', as in the film, where Captain Kirk uses his 'communicator' to give orders to other crew members on the spaceship Enterprise. Cooper's device became the world's first handheld mobile phone, and from 1973, it was being sold worldwide.

It therefore seems that if we want to know which new technologies ________________ ___________________ (6) (*make*) a big impact on everyday life by the end of this century, we need to take a closer look at the inventions created by science-fiction writers. H.G. Wells' novel about time travel, *The Time Machine* (1895), has been seen as pure fantasy, but perhaps in the future, time travel ______________________ __________ (7) (*become*) as common as using a mobile phone today.

23 **In ten years' time.** Use the words to form sentences with the future perfect.

1 I | finish | university | in ten years' time

____.

2 I hope | I | learn | to be | more tolerant | by the time I'm thirty

____.

3 We | invent | a way to live | on Mars | by 2050

____.

4 In ten years' time | I | buy | my first driverless car

____.

5 We | not replace | mobile phones | before the end of the century

____.

24 Emails to my future self

a Read three emails teenagers have written to their future selves and answer the questions.

1 Why do the teenagers decide to write emails to their future selves?
2 What do you learn from emails A – C about each teenager's personality and interests?

A – *Sent to me 5 years in the future*

Dear Future me! I hope you're remembering to eat healthily and exercise at least twice a week, Jessie. Maybe you will have got better at doing yoga and will be able to do the poses that you couldn't do when you were 14. I hope so! If not, you should probably stop doing yoga! I hope that you will have managed to stay in touch with the friends you had five years ago. Remember that you can always call or text them any time.
Love, Old me

B – *Sent to me 15 years in the future*

Hi 30-year-old Carla! How are you doing, old lady? Can you believe how old you are now? Just because you're old doesn't mean you have to stop having fun though. My wish for you is that you aren't working too hard. I hope that you will have found a really interesting job, but you also need to enjoy yourself. Remember you love climbing, running and swimming – so there are three ideas for things to do in your free time if you can't think of anything.
Love you, 15-year-old Carla

C – *Sent to me 11 years in the future*

Hey Future Paul! You must be 25 now. I really believe in you and that you will have achieved your dream of becoming a doctor. I know how determined you are to succeed and how hard you will have studied to make that dream come true. I'm sure you will already have started thinking about how you can do more to help people or get a more senior job at the hospital. Keep up the good work and never stop trying your best!
Past Paul

b Read the emails again and answer these questions.

1 What change does Jessie think will have happened in her life in five years' time?
2 What does Carla hope won't have happened by the time she's 30 years old?
3 Why does Paul think he will have achieved something that's important to him before his 25th birthday?

>>> **c** You're going to write an email to your future self. Make notes on the following points and then use your notes to write your email (about 80 – 120 words).

- The time in the future when you want your future self to receive the email.
- The reason for writing to your future self.
- What changes you think will have happened in your life by that point in time and what will have stayed the same.
- What you think your future self might need to hear or might need to be reminded of.

25 READING FOCUS: International Space Station

The International Space Station is a large satellite. Inside, the space station, there is a large laboratory for experiments and accommodation where six astronauts can live for several months. It is 72.8 metres long and 20 metres high, so it's roughly the same size as a small block of flats.
The construction of the space station was an international effort, and engineers from the United States, Europe, Russia, Japan and Canada worked on it. One hundred and fifty-nine components were manufactured and then joined together to create the space station. Since its launch in 1998, the International Space Station has been orbiting the Earth at a speed of 7.66 kilometres per second, which means it can orbit the Earth in just 92 minutes. So if you were living in the space station and looking out of the windows, you would be able to see the sun rising and setting sixteen times a day!

a Read about the International Space Station. Match the amounts with the things they refer to.

1 six
2 almost seventy-three
3 twenty
4 almost one hundred and sixty
5 just over 7.6 km/s
6 ninety-two

a the height of the space station in metres
b the number of minutes that it takes the space station to travel around the Earth
c the number of people who can stay on the space station at one time
d the speed at which the space station travels around the Earth
e the length of the space station in metres
f the number of parts that the space station is made of

b Read the text again. Match the words with their definitions.

1 several
2 roughly
3 effort
4 component
5 to orbit
6 to set

a not exactly
b a part of something
c more than one; usually two, three or four
d hard work completed to achieve an objective
e to go down, when talking about the sun
f to travel around in a circle

>>> **c** Do some research about another satellite or space station – past or present. Find facts or figures similar to those in **a** and use them to write a short text (150 words).

Present your product or service

26 The business plan

a The students whose idea you saw on page 68 have made some changes after realizing some possible problems with their business plan. Read the new plan. What four changes have they made to their original one?

Our business idea is called *Bike 2 U* and it's a mobile bike repair service. It solves the problem that it can be difficult or inconvenient to transport a broken bike to a repair shop by sending the mechanics to repair the bike at the customer's home. The mechanics will travel in a van so they can easily transport any equipment they need for the repairs and even take the bike to a central workshop if necessary.
The service will be available from early in the morning until the evening seven days a week, so customers are sure to find a time that suits them. However, we will ensure that more mechanics are available in the evenings and at weekends because those are the times when our target customers – young people who ride bikes – are most likely to be at home. We will only need to rent a small workshop to do some of the work as most repairs will be done at the customer's home. Our mechanics will receive a similar salary to those who work in bike repair shops to help us recruit some of the best mechanics for our company.

b Imagine that you had thought of the *Bike 2 U* business idea. Prepare a presentation with a partner about it using visual aids. Remember to:

- create a hook to get the listeners' attention at the start of the presentation.
- tell the audience what you're going to talk about in the presentation.
- explain the problem that this service solves and how it does that.
- explain your target market and why these customers will be interested in your service.
- explain what makes your service special or different to other similar services.

USEFUL PHRASES

Have you ever ...?
Imagine that you ...
Picture this situation: ...
Our plan is to ...

We want to show you how you can ...
We've come up with a solution: ...
The best part about it is that ...
And that's not all, ...

People will want to buy our product / use our service because ...
Customers will love this because ...

c Watch another pair's presentation and make notes on the answers to the following questions.

1 How well do they know their product / service?
2 Do they tell a good story about their product / service?
3 Do they use visual aids effectively?
4 Do they show how their idea is different?
5 Do they show how the customer will benefit?

d Use te feedback from **c** to improve your presentation and give it to another pair.

Mediation

27 Young inventors

a Your English exchange partner Jamie is discussing innovations at school. You found an interesting article. Write an email to Jamie (100 – 120 words) and present the three innovations you have read about in the article.

Erfindungen von Kindern

[...] Das Trampolin
Die Idee für das Trampolin kam dem 16-jährigen George Nissen 1930 bei einem Ausflug in den Zirkus. Ihm gefiel es, wie sich die Trapeztänzer am Ende in ein großes Netz fallen ließen. Da er schon von klein auf begeisterter Turner [...] war, stellte er sich ein neues Sportgerät vor, auf dem man tolle Sprünge machen könnte. Zuhause in der Garage baute Nissen sein erstes Trampolin. Der Name Trampolin kommt vom spanischen Wort „el trampolín“ ([...] *Sprungbrett*). Das Trampolin wurde vor allem während des 2. Weltkrieges bekannt, wo es zur Vorbereitung für Piloten und Fallschirmspringer diente.

Popsicle, oder auch: Eis am Stiel

An einem Abend im Jahr 1905 in den USA wollte sich der elfjährige Frank Epperson Limo mit Brausepulver machen. Er mischte alles zusammen und rührte mit einem Holzstäbchen um. Da ihm die Limo nicht kalt genug war, stellte er sie zum Abkühlen nach draußen. Der junge Epperson vergaß sein Getränk und da es Winter war, fror die Limonade über Nacht ein. Am nächsten Tag holte er die gefrorene Limo herein. Im warmen Zimmer löste sich das Eis vom Rand des Bechers und Frank hatte ein Eis am Stiel in der Hand. Erst Jahre später meldete er ein Patent für die „Popsicles“ [...] an und verkaufte die ersten auf einer Party.

Die Ohrenschützer
Im Winter 1873 in den USA ging der 15-jährige Chester Greenwood Schlittschuhlaufen. Dabei hatte er einen Schal um den Kopf gewickelt, denn die damaligen Wollmützen kratzten ihn zu sehr. Der Schal verrutschte allerdings immer wieder und Chester fror an den Ohren. Da kam ihm die Idee für Ohrenschützer. Er bog einige Drahtreifen zurecht und bat dann seine Oma, echtes Fell als Polsterung für die Ohren darauf zu nähen. 1877 ließ er seine Erfindung patentieren und verdiente damit sehr viel Geld. [...]

www.kindersache.de

b After Jamie read your email, he did some research and found an article about Richie Stachowski, a boy who became an inventor at the age of ten. Jamie sent you the article. Your brother thinks the picture is funny and asks you what it is about. Tell him about Richie Stachowski, what his innovations were and how he came up with the idea for them.

Richie Stachowski (Age 10) – Water Talkie

In 1996, 10-year-old Richie Stachowski went on a trip to Hawaii with his family. 'I was surfing with my dad. When we dove under, there were so many beautiful things to see. I wished we could talk underwater,' he said. After finding out that there were no inventions for this kind of sub-aquatic communication, Stachowski started researching underwater acoustics and tried out prototypes in the family pool and the public pool, too. He got the pool management staff interested and they let him tinker away. Eventually, he came up with the Water Talkie – a conical device with a blow valve and plastic membrane that enables swimmers to talk to each other underwater from as far as 15 feet away.

Next, Stachowski went to New Jersey and pitched his idea to a big toy company. At the end of the interview, he had an order for 50,000 units. With the help of his mom, Stachowski started a company called Short Stack LLC (named in honor of his love of pancakes) and went on to invent other successful pool toys. In 1999, at age 13, he sold his company.

My review

1 About technological developments
1 have been transformed
2 are controlled
3 are connected
4 have been invented
5 will be done
6 have already been lost
7 have been taken over
8 were launched
9 were sold
10 are used

2 About the climate
1 had enjoyed
2 wouldn't have thrown
3 hadn't forgotten
4 would have come
5 had known
6 wouldn't have used
7 hadn't left
8 would have shown
9 had prepared
10 would have been

3 About presenting and discussing arguments
1 I agree with
2 Sorry to interrupt, but
3 Exactly
4 I don't agree
5 I'm not finished
6 Go ahead
7 That may be, but
8 That might be true
9 You have a point

4 About the future
1 will be faced
2 will be
3 will have risen
4 will mean
5 will have disappeared
6 will have had
7 won't happen
8 will have experienced
9 will have died
10 will have become
11 will have found

Dream big

1 My future

25 **a** Listen to three friends talking about their plans for the future. Fill in the missing words in sentences 1–3 and then answer questions 4 and 5.

1 Ava is good at ______________________ and she's interested in ______________________.

2 Brandon isn't keen ______________________ and he isn't good at ______________________, but he's good at ______________________.

3 Avery is good at ______________________ and she loves ______________________.

4 What's Ava's problem and what advice does Brandon give her?

____

______________________.

5 What problem does Brandon have?

____

______________________.

b Read the information on page 84 from an online guide. Which careers would be the most suitable for Ava, Avery and Brandon? Give reasons for your choices.

Ava ______________________

____

Avery ______________________

____

Brandon ______________________

____

2 Subject choices

26 **a** After a few days, Ava, Avery and Brandon meet again. Listen to the first part of their conversation and answer the questions.

1 What has Ava found and where has she found it?
2 Why does Avery think it is useful?
3 What has Avery decided? Why?

Economics

Economics involves studying areas of politics, sociology, law, psychology and history.
Our degree combines economic theory with investigation. Candidates should be good at math and IT, show an ability to analyse problems and have an understanding of current affairs.
As a professional economist, you may find positions in local and national government departments, banks, multinational companies, financial consultancy companies and accountancy firms.

Communication and Journalism

Communication is the essence of today's digital, virtual organizations. If you're interested in learning about professional communication, improving your written and verbal communication skills, and developing in-depth knowledge and values for the workplace, our combined programme is the option for you. You can specialize in print, digital or broadcast journalism and focus on corporate communication and marketing, public relations or social media communication.

Science

Do you have an enquiring mind and an interest in scientific developments? Do you have problem-solving, numerical and IT skills? Are you good at math, geography, chemistry, biology or physics? Then maybe you should consider a career in Science. You may start with a core science or study a more specialist subject, for example biomedical science, genetics, marine biology or astrophysics. Depending on your field of study and your specialization, this could lead to a job in research and development, the pharmacology industry, space research or the nuclear industry.

Art

Are you wondering what careers exist for those who study creative subjects at high school? While becoming an architect, fine artist, sculptor or gallery assistant is always an option, there are many other jobs available as diverse as graphic or 3D product designer, special-effects designer or makeup artist, comic illustrator, marine photographer or web designer.

Earth Sciences

If you're good at math, geography, physics, chemistry and biology and want to learn more about climate change, pollution and conservation, then you should consider a degree in Earth Sciences. There are four major areas of Earth Science: geology, oceanography, astronomy and meteorology. Graduates are in great demand to develop new sources of energy, to find new metal and other mineral resources, or to study water cycles and atmospheric patterns. Job prospects are excellent.

Click on the links to check which colleges offer courses in these subjects.

27

b Listen to the second part of the conversation and complete the sentences.

1 Ava decided ______________________________.

2 She reconsidered her decision because ______________________________.

3 Brandon suggested ______________________________ because ______________________________.

4 Brandon decided ______________________________.

3 **A career counsellor.** Listen to an interview with Dr Jackson and answer the questions.

28

1 What qualifications does a person need to work as a counsellor?
2 How is a counselling interview conducted?
3 What does she point out as important to remember in a counselling interview?

Practice: Careers of the future

4 Salary or job satisfaction?

a Read the quote. Do you agree with it? Give reasons for your answer.

> Choose a job you love, and you will never have to work a day in your life. *Confucius*

b List the factors that you think are important in achieving 'job satisfaction'. Justify your opinions.

5 Dr Jackson's advice

29 **a** Listen to the end of the interview with Dr Jackson and do the tasks.

1 List the positive and negative effects related to job choice that she makes.

____

____.

2 Summarize Dr Jackson's opinion.

____

____

____.

b Rewrite each sentence so it means the same as the first. Be careful with the prepositions!

1 I could go to university, but I'm not sure I want to study for at least four years.

I have thought ____________ university, but I'm not sure I like the idea ____________ for at least four years.

2 I want to take a gap year and work to earn money for university.

My reason ____________ a gap year is to earn money for university.

3 Why volunteer? Why work for no money?

I'm not keen ____________. What's the advantage ____________ for no money?

4 I can't make up my mind. One day I want to study biology, the next I definitely want to work with kids.

I'm not good ____________ decisions. One day I'm interested ____________ biology, the next I'm passionate ____________ with kids.

5 I can't wait to leave school, but I'm scared I might make the wrong decision about my future.

I'm really looking forward ____________ school, but I'm afraid ____________ the wrong decision about my future.

6 READING FOCUS: What matters more?

What matters more?

It is clear that a high salary and job satisfaction are two of the most important reasons why people choose a career. However, they may not always come together and sometimes you have to make a choice. Some people are satisfied with a high salary even if they do not like the job. Others are happy doing what they love, even if their monthly account balance is far from ideal.

It's a fact that there are personal factors that influence the choices people make. Our responsibilities define our lifestyles, so it is natural to feel money is more important than than job satisfaction. When your basic needs are covered, you can start thinking about factors like work-life balance and job satisfaction. If you know that your bills are always catered for, you are more likely to stay in that job, whether you enjoy it or not.

According to research, the main motivation to change jobs is the search for better pay, but it varies according to the level of income. In countries where the average salary is low, 76% of the population say that they would definitely change their job if they were offered a better salary, whereas in wealthier countries this figure changes significantly. In Britain, the percentage drops to 42.2%. While in the US, almost 70% of people making more than $150,000 per year reported being 'very satisfied' with their current job and did not consider changing. Only 40% making under $50,000 said the same.

Another personal factor that influences our priorities is age. Young people apparently value company culture more than previous generations. Young employees seem to be choosing job satisfaction over money, and many are willing to give up a high salary in exchange for a healthier working environment. Most of them are likely to spend more time at work than with family and friends, and they think that if they aren't happy in their job, life could get quite stressful and it's simply not worth it.

However, while that is true, sometimes it's just not possible. It can take time to find the 'perfect' job, and you may need to do something else to keep you going for a short while. That doesn't mean you are going to give up on your dreams completely and work in a job you hate until you retire, but it's okay to put them on hold for a while. It may be hard to work in a full-time job you don't enjoy, but if you have enough determination, you'll be able to make it happen.

a Read the article and decide if Dr Jackson would agree with it. Explain your reasons.

____

____

____

b What is the writer's opinion? How does he support it?

____

____

c According to the article, what is the best thing to do? Do you agree? Justify your opinion.

____

____

____

____

____

____

d Explain the meaning of the following phrases.

1 their monthly account balance is far from ideal

____

2 work-life balance

____

3 your bills are always catered for

____

4 to give up on your dreams

____

5 to put them on hold

____

7 Your career

a Add the missing prepositions to these expressions.

be good	______	dream	______
be interested	______	get used	______
be excellent	______	have the chance	______
be responsible	______	specialize	______

b Write 80 – 120 words about your future career. Use the questions below as a guide and the expessions you completed in **a**.

- Why have you chosen it?
- What skills, qualities and qualifications are necessary?
- What job prospects does it offer?
- What would you be willing to give up if necessary?
- Would an intelligent machine be able to replace you in your future job? Why or why not?

to dream of ■ to enjoy ■ to specialize in ■ excellent / good at ■ interested in ■ responsible for ■ to be an expert in ■ to get used to ■ to have the chance of

→ students' book, pages 114/115

My part-time job

8 Pros and cons

30 **a** Some people argue that part-time jobs are good for teenagers. Others think that they are problematic. Listen to the interviews in a shopping centre and make notes about what each person thinks.

Emma ______________________________

______________________________.

Man ______________________________

______________________________.

Francisco ______________________________

______________________________.

Teff ______________________________

______________________________.

b Emma listened to all of the interviews and when she returned home, she told her parents about them. Rewrite the sentences.

1 I think working part-time is a good idea.
I told the presenter ______________________________.

2 I've worked part-time for the last three years.
I added ______________________________.

3 I've done different jobs.
I mentioned ______________________________.

4 I don't think kids should work.
A man said ______________________________.

5 I wouldn't allow my children to have a part-time job.
He added ______________________________.

6 I think it's a very good thing to have a part-time job.
A boy disagreed and said he ______________________________.

7 A job gives you experience dealing with people.
He explained ______________________________.

8 We've both worked part-time and we have good marks.
His sister added ______________________________.

30 **c** Listen again and outline the pros and cons of part-time jobs.

PROS	CONS

9 What do you think?

30 **a** Listen to the interviews in **8** again. Which of the speakers do you agree with most? Explain why and give examples.

____

____

____

b Prepare to talk about your position with a partner. Here are a few useful phrases:

- In my opinion, the man ...
- I'm convinced that ...
- Another way of looking at this ...
- I agree / I don't agree that ...
- What I'm saying is ...
- ... said that ..., but I think ...

c Take notes of your partner's opinions. Then write a short summary of what he / she has said.

10 Teff's job.
Teff has been looking at some part-time jobs for the summer and she has found one she's interested in. Report what she told her brother. Vary the reporting verbs.

1 I have found an interesting ad about a non-residential summer school.

______________________________.

2 They need students to work with children on the summer courses in July and August.

______________________________.

3 They are looking for students older than 15.

______________________________.

4 They will need instructors for tennis, swimming, music and art.

______________________________.

5 They will pay transport and we can have lunch and refreshments for free.

______________________________.

→ students' book, pages 116/117

Practice: Student jobbing

11 Part-time jobs

a Read the information about part-time jobs in Germany and decide if these people can do the jobs they have found. Explain why or why not.

Youth Labour Laws
What is the legal working age in Germany?

The *Jugendarbeitsschutzgesetz* (Youth Labour Protection Laws) applies to teenagers between 15 and 18 years old.

The earliest age somebody can start working in Germany is 13, with parental permission, but this option is extremely limited.

Children younger than 14 can help in the house, but are not allowed to work outside the family home and are required to attend school five days per week.

Teenagers cannot do any job that could endanger his or her physical or mental health.

Children under 16 can't work between 20.00 and 06.00.
Teenagers older than 16 may work until 23.00 in restaurants and bars, from 05.00 in bakeries and on farms. On farms, they can also work until 21.00.

Teenagers older than 17 are permitted to begin work at 04.00 in bakeries.

Teenagers are not allowed to work on Saturdays and Sundays during the academic year and they must have at least two Saturdays and two Sundays per month off.

1 Johan (12): deliver newspapers for local newsagent

2 Marina (13): babysit for neighbour, Saturdays, 21.00 – 23.00

3 Raj (15): basketball coach at children's camp, weekends, 9.00 – 11.00, July

4 Sonja (17): waitress, Monday – Friday, 17.00 – 22.00, July – August

5 Ada (16): baker's assistant, Saturday – Sunday, 9.00 – 12.00, September – December

b Listen to the information about finding a summer job in Germany and do the tasks.

1 Indicate the number of hours regular students can work during the holidays and during the academic year.
2 Comment on the situation of non-EEA students.
3 List the most popular jobs.
4 Describe what an au pair has to do and what benefits they have.
5 According to the advisor, what should foreign students remember? Why?

12 Summer jobs around the world

a Read the text about summer jobs in Morocco. Then put sentences 1 – 5 in the correct place in the text.

1 They don't need to work, but they want to add to their personal experience and prepare themselves for future employment.
2 She has been able to build a small customer base who appreciate her culinary skills.
3 Most come from families with limited incomes so they have to give up their holidays.
4 Sociologists say that Moroccan society is changing, especially in big cities, because everyone has understood the importance of education.
5 His father died when he was six and he sells whatever he can carry on his back and in his arms.

Jobs in Morocco

Many students in Morocco have to work during the summer to fund their studies the following year. ☐ (1) Some of them may sell boxes of tissues in the city streets or ice cream on the beach. For five years, 14-year-old Aamir has had to be financially self-sufficient. ☐ (2) His mother worked as a cleaner, but she couldn't meet the family's needs, so Aamir asked her to allow him to work during the summer. He says, 'I don't want to give up on my studies because it's the only way I can make progress and be better off when I grow up. I want my mother to stop working and have some rest.'
Anisaa is 16 years old and very skilful at making traditional biscuits and sweets. ☐ (3) 'My dad is a seasonal worker and my mum is a housewife. I have three younger brothers and it's difficult for my parents to make a living, so I decided to take my future into my own hands and work during my free time. Now Dad doesn't have to worry so much about money.
Other young people whose families are better off also choose to work during the holidays. ☐ (4) For two years, Hadiya, 18, has worked as a cashier in July. At first, her parents, who are doctors at the local hospital, were surprised and not sure they should let their daughter work in a supermarket. She explained why she wanted to do it and they agreed. She says, 'My work has helped my self-confidence. Besides, the money I earn this month means I will be able to go on holiday to Spain in August.'
Some university students work as secretaries for lawyers, dentists and doctors whose employees are on holiday. Some students even teach private lessons to school students who need to sit for exams. ☐ (5) More and more parents are convinced that working during the holidays will teach their children how to become more responsible.

b Read the text again and find words in the text that match these definitions.

1 to provide the money for something that costs a lot ____________________
2 money that someone gets from working ____________________
3 to stop doing something that you do regularly ____________________
4 in a better situation, e.g. having more money ____________________

c Report what Aamir and Anisaa say.

1 I don't want to give up on my studies because it's the only way I can make progress and be better off when I grow up.

Aamir said ______________________________

______________________________.

2 I want my mother to stop working and have some rest.

He added ______________________________.

3 My dad is a seasonal worker and my mum is a housewife.

Anisaa said ______________________________.

4 I have three younger brothers and it's difficult for my parents to make a living, so I decided to take my future into my own hands and work during my free time.

She explained ______________________________.

5 Now Dad doesn't have to worry so much about money.

She mentioned ______________________________.

13 VIEWING FOCUS: Non-verbal communication

3 **a** What you do with your body during a conversation is just as important as the words you say. Watch these people decide what messages they are communicating. Then answer the questions.

1 What's the difference between the two conversations between Tom and Deb in scene 1?

______________________________.

2 How is Tom feeling in the two situations? Why is Deb reacting the way she is?

______________________________.

3 If you were Deb in scene 2, what would you do differently?

______________________________.

3 **b** Watch scene 2 again. According to your answers in **a**, video yourself acting out the situation.

c Write a short script for two scenes where non-verbal communication completely changes the messages you want to communicate. Act them out with a partner and video yourselves. Show the class and discuss how non-verbal communication affects the messages. Make some notes here.

____

____

____

____

Create a storyboard

14 A student documentary

32 **a** A group of students from Aurora, Illinois are making a documentary. Listen to them and explain what they are planning to do and why.

____

____

____

33 **b** Listen to the second part of the conversation and do the tasks.

1 List the places they are going to show.

____

______________________________.

2 Explain how long the documentary will be and why.

____

______________________________.

3 Describe how they are going to start the documentary.

____

______________________________.

4 Outline what they have forgotten to plan. How will they solve the problem?

____

______________________________.

c You have heard the details of the documentary. Now write a one-line summary for it.

____

15 Planning your documentary

a You are going to make a 10 – 15 minute documentary about your city. Plan what it will be about, in what order you will present the information and what you will need (*locations*, *people*, *permission*, etc.).

____

____

b Now write a one-line summary.

____

Summer jobs

16 What do you have to do?

a Read the job posts on a website for teenagers and answer the questions.

Lifeguard

If you are 15+ and a very good swimmer, this may be the job for you.
We need a certified lifeguard for a summer camp swimming pool.
9 a.m. – 1 p.m. Sat – Sun.
£30 per weekend + lunch and bus fare.
Call Seaview Summer Camp on 094 567 32 19.

Babysitter needed (girls only)

We need a responsible young and energetic person (15+) to look after our three children aged 5, 7 and 9.
2 p.m. – 5 p.m., Mon – Fri, £45 a week.
Basic knowledge of first aid and fluent in German an advantage.
Call Gertrude on 678 93 92 00.

City Museum Shop

Are you 16+? Do you want to earn some extra money?
We need French, Spanish or German speakers.
Tuesday – Saturday, 9 a.m. – 5 p.m. throughout August.
Send your CV to: citymuseum@shopjob.lkj.

Greg's Café

We are looking for breakfast and lunchtime staff (16+).
7.30 a.m. – 3 p.m. on Saturdays in July and August.
Call Bella on 612 39 87 45 (after 4 p.m.) for an interview.
Previous experience an advantage, breakfast and lunch provided.
Fluent French or Spanish and advantage.

1 In which job do you only need to work on Saturdays? ______
2 Which job is not for boys? ______
3 Which job lasts for just a month? ______
4 In which job do you have to speak a foreign language? ______
5 Which job starts the earliest? ______
6 In which job do you have to have certification? ______

b Read the candidate profiles and match each person to the most suitable job.

Oliver – 16
Loves children, has two sisters.
Previous experience babysitting.
First aid certification.
Bilingual in English and German. Responsible.
Interested in History and Literature.
Job: ______________________________

Maria – 15
Winner of school swimming competition.
Responsible and energetic.
Available weekday afternoons.
Doing the lifeguard certificate.
Job: ______________________________

Suri – 16
Fluent French and English.
Turkish first language.
Good at sports.
Loves art and music.
Plays cello and bass guitar.
Only free on Saturdays.
Job: ______________________________

Antonia – 17
Bilingual in English and Spanish.
Free at weekends.
Lifeguard certificate completed. Good with children.
Loves telling stories.
Job: ______________________________

17 A job interview

a Imagine you were being interviewed for one of the jobs on page 94. Complete the interview.

Interviewer How did you learn about this job?

You ____.

Interviewer Yes, it's a part-time job. ________________ hours a week, ________________.
Do you have any experience in this kind of job?

You ____.

Interviewer I see in your application that you ______________________________.
Could you tell me more about that?

You ____.

Interviewer Do you have any questions?

You ____.

____.

Interviewer We would be delighted to offer you the job.

b Later, you are telling your parents about the interview. Report the conversation.

____

____

____

____.

→ students' book, pages 122/123

Practice: Into the world

18 **Volunteering.** Have you ever thought about going on a volunteer programme? Why or why not? What would you expect a volunteer programme to offer? Write about 100 words.

19 **Anja's volunteering experience.** Anja is a high school student and she's done voluntary work. Listen and do the tasks and answer the questions.

34

1 Summarize Anja's experience. Explain where she went, what she did and the challenges she faced. ____.

2 Why does she mention retired people? ____.

3 Why are young people more interested in doing voluntary work nowadays? __________________.

4 What skills does it help develop? ____.

5 According to Anja, what does facing challenges teach you? __________________________.

20 **Around the world**

a Read about volunteer programmes around the world on page 97. Find words and phrases that match these definitions.

1 to pay for expenses ____________

2 money given for a specific purpose ____________

3 to join a course or organization ____________

4 money for spending on your own personal things ____________

5 causing little or no damage to the environment ____________

6 to train as you do the job ____________

7 a large number of different plants and animals in a particular area ____________

Government to launch volunteer programme

The government is launching a programme for young adults who would like to work with aid organizations in developing countries. This is in response to an increasing demand from those who want to help in developing countries but do not know how to go about it or finance their stay abroad. 10,000 places will be offered each year and the programme will receive annual funding of € 54 million.
Adults aged 18 – 30 can sign up for volunteer programmes in Africa, Asia and Latin America from 6 to 24 months. Participants will receive a monthly stipend of € 600 to cover travel costs, training and insurance as well as some pocket money. Candidates must be in possession of a high school diploma or similar.
The programme includes working with street educators and local volunteers providing shelter and food, running literacy classes with street children, promoting artistic activities with children in rural areas, working on ecological projects and providing assistance to people with disabilities.

The organic farm experience

Would you like to learn about organic farming for two months? Our movement links volunteers with organic farmers to promote cultural and educational experiences helping to build a sustainable, global community.
Our Organic Farmer Volunteer Programme will give you the opportunity to learn about organic agriculture and sustainability by helping and living with farmers. No previous experience of farming needed! You will learn as you go!
You're expected to help with daily tasks such as taking care of the animals, gardening, making or repairing fences and cooking. Farmers are happy to share their knowledge, stories, traditions and recipes.
Our programme will provide you with a connection to a new community in a natural environment surrounded by people from all over the world.

Destination Costa Rica!

Costa Rica is famous for its progressive environmental and social policies and it is considered one of the planet's most sustainable countries. It is home to a rich variety of plants and animals, it contains 5 % of the world's biodiversity and is home to over 200 species of mammals and 800 species of birds.
The most important requirements for the programme are being ecologically minded, willing to learn about new cultures, enthusiastic, hard-working and willing to give up between two weeks and two months of your time.
Candidates must be fit and healthy and ready to work outdoors. Jobs include cleaning animal cages, preparing the food for the animals, always under supervision and with strict security measures in some cases, learning how to work with animals and helping to develop special projects. New ideas are always welcome!
If you are 18 or older, have a keen interest in animal conservation, an open mind and a flexible attitude, then this is the programme for you!

b Tick (✓) the programmes from page 97 which include the following.

		Government Volunteering Programme	Organic Farm Experience	Destination Costa Rica!
1	You will be in contact with nature.	☐	☐	☐
2	It can last up to two years.	☐	☐	☐
3	You can join for two or three weeks.	☐	☐	☐
4	You will teach.	☐	☐	☐
5	It doesn't have an age limit.	☐	☐	☐
6	You can work with animals.	☐	☐	☐
7	You can learn how to cook.	☐	☐	☐
8	You have to be fit.	☐	☐	☐
9	There are special security measures.	☐	☐	☐
10	You will learn about a different lifestyle.	☐	☐	☐

21 **SPEAKING FOCUS: Volunteer programmes**

35 **a** Luka has been on an EU volunteer programme and he's giving a talk about it to a group of students. Listen and take notes on the most important points.

____

____

____

____

____

b What questions would you like to ask him? Would you be interested in registering for this programme? Explain your answer.

____

____

____

____

22 **Look for information about volunteering programmes in your country.** Choose one and make notes for a one-minute talk. Think of possible questions your classmates may ask and include the information.

Children's rights

23 The rights of the child

a Complete the text with the correct quantifiers. Sometimes more than one answer is possible.

a few ■ all ■ both ■ many ■ most

According to the UN Convention on the Rights of the Child (UNCRC), a child is anyone under the age of 18. They have the same general human rights as adults and specific rights that recognize their special needs. ________________ (1) the EU and ________________ (2) EU countries must respect, protect and fulfil the rights of the child. The Charter of Fundamental Rights guarantees the protection of the rights of the child by the EU institutions and countries. ________________ (3) Article 24 and Article 32 specifically cover children's rights.

As UNICEF explains, the Convention on the Rights of the Child recognizes the fundamental human dignity of ________________ (4) children and the urgency of ensuring their well-being and development. It makes clear that a basic quality of life should be the right of ________________ (5) children, rather than the privilege of ________________ (6).

________________ (7) areas of a country's government policy affect children to some degree, therefore, policymaking that does not take children into account has a negative impact on the future of ________________ (8) members of society.

________________ (9) changes in society are having a negative impact on children. Globalization, climate change, digitalization, mass migration, changes in employment patterns and an increasingly reduced social welfare system in ________________ (10) countries ________________ (11) impact on children. This impact can be particularly damaging in situations of war and natural disaster.

The healthy development of children is crucial to the future well-being of any society. Children are especially vulnerable to poor living conditions, inadequate health care, lack of safe water and pollution. In ________________ (12) countries around the world, living conditions threaten the future of children and the societies in which they live.

b Read the text again and do the tasks.

1. Summarize the main points of the text.
2. Explain how a country's policy can negatively affect children's rights.
3. Comment on how climate change is likely to affect children's rights in the future.

»» **c** Find out what Articles 24 and 32 of the Charter of Fundamental Rights are about and summarize the main points.

24 Child labour: facts and figures

36 a Your class are learning about children's rights. Listen to the radio programme and make some notes. Then complete the sentences. Use the correct quantifiers from the box.

few ■ a little ■ many ■ most of ■ one fifth ■ the majority

1 _______________ the children who live in Asia have to work under dangerous circumstances and _______________ of them are victims of child abuse and exploitation.

2 In sub-Saharan Africa, _______________ of the child population has to work.

3 In spite of India's economic growth, only _______________ people have benefitted from this growth.

4 The _______________ of Indian children move to bigger cities for work.

5 Unemployment and cuts in social aid have meant that _______________ families to send their children to work.

6 Only _______________ information on child labour in Europe is available. _______________ countries agree to send their reports.

b Explain the reasons why child labour still exists in Europe.

____

____

____

36 c Listen again and list the jobs most commonly done by children mentioned in the interview.

____

____

d In your opinion, why would some countries refuse to give information on child labour?

____

____

____

____

____

____

Practice: Stand up for children's rights

25 Children in India

Children in India

Asha-Kiran, which means 'Ray of Light' in Hindi, is a small NGO (non-governmental organization) based in Spain and founded by Uttam Módenes and Paloma Sousa (Hansa). They started by establishing Day Care Centres and the Yashodhara Home, and they have developed many projects in India.
Day Care Centres specialize in the care and schooling of the children of migrant construction workers. In India, construction is the biggest source of employment for migrant workers who wander from town to town in search for work. The children of these workers, about 30 million, roam the streets near the construction sites or play among the rubble. The majority of children find it difficult to enrol in conventional schools because they often do not speak the local language and because they remain in each place for a limited time. Therefore, they begin to work in construction at an early age, contributing to increasing rates of child labour.
The Yashodara Home offers vulnerable children a place to live. Through this project, they have access to health and hygiene, access to education and vocational training, and the chance to live in an environment where the protection of their rights is guaranteed. Asha-Kiran has also started a partnership with New Vision NGO and Rainbow Homes to offer protection to the most vulnerable sector of society: street girls. Due to their gender, girls in India are the most deprived. The majority are orphans or do not have stable homes, they are often forced to beg and are victims of violence. That is why the Rainbow Homes project cooperates with local authorities in order to support the programme. The Young Promises project offers educational opportunities to young people so that they can continue with their studies. The children the foundation has been working with for a long time have grown up, have become responsible and wish to continue their studies. The project revolves around the following areas: education, health care and working with families, so they can improve their quality of life and support their children with their education.

a Your class has found some information about an organization which works with children in India. Find words in the text that have these meanings and highlight them.

1 to go from place to place without a direction or purpose
2 broken pieces of stone and brick from buildings, walls, etc.
3 not having the things that are essential for a comfortable life
4 to ask people for money because you are very poor
5 someone attacked or harmed by a criminal

b Complete these sentences with four of the words from **a**.

1 The robbers attacked four people. Later one ____________________ died in hospital.

2 Many children in India have a ____________________ childhood, often without enough to eat.

3 Even in Germany, some people have to ________________ for money or food.

4 After the earthquake, the children played in the ____________________ while their parents tried to rebuild their lives.

»» **c** Look for information about an NGO in your region and write 150 words describing their aims and work.

26 37 **A biography.** Listen to a radio programme about Om Prakash Gurjar. Then complete the summary of his biography.

Date of birth: ____________ Place of birth: ____________

Education: ____________

Timeline: ____________

Awards: ____________

27 **WRITING FOCUS: Kailash Satyarthi.** Kailash Satyarthi is an Indian social reformer who campaigned against child labour in India and for the universal right to education. Use the notes to write his biography (150 words).

Name: Kailash Satyarthi
Date of birth: 11 January 1954
Place of birth: Vidisha, Madhya Pradesh, India
Family: middle class, one brother, father policeman
Education: Government Boys Higher Secondary School, Vidisha; degree in Electrical Engineering, Samrat Ashok Technological Institute; post-graduate degree in High-voltage Engineering; college lecturer, Bhopal

Timeline:
1980 founded the Bachpan Bachao Andolan (Save Childhood Movement)
founded the International Center on Child Labor and Education
1998 led the Global March against Child Labour across 103 countries
1999 formed and became president of the Global Campaign for Education
2004 established the Kailash Satyarthi Children's Foundation (KSCF)
2015 developed agenda for the United Nation's Sustainable Development Goals

Awards:
1994 The Aachener International Peace Award (Germany)
1995 Robert F. Kennedy Human Rights Award (US)
2007 recognized in US State Dept list of 'Heroes Acting to End Modern Day Slavery'
2014 Nobel Peace Prize

Shoot and edit your film material

28 A shooting schedule

a Four students from Aurora, Illinois, are ready to make a detailed shooting schedule. Listen, choose two of the five scenes, and complete the chart.

Project: Documentary about Aurora

Date / Time		
Scene		
Shot		
Location		
What happens? How?		
What to think of?		

b In what order are they going to film the shots? Why have they planned it this way?

____

____

____

29 Shoot your film

a Write the shooting schedule for the documentary about your city that you planned on page 93. You can also include a map to show the locations.

b Shoot your film and evaluate it. Does it show the planned steps? Is the sound clear? Is the light good enough?

c Edit your film and present your film to the class.

Mediation

30 **Camp Adventure.** You and your English friend Sarah want to spend a holiday together. At the moment Sarah is visiting you. You have a look at the following website. Sarah's German isn't very good. Answer her questions.

Camp Adventure

Camp Adventure ist eine Organisation des Gründers Jan Vieth, die seit 2002 die positiven Aspekte von deutschen Ferienfreizeiten mit denen kanadischer Sommercamps verbindet, um Kindern und Jugendlichen aus aller Welt ein tolles Abenteuersport-Ferienlager zu bieten. Seit 2015 bieten wir auch erlebnispädagogische Klassenreisen in unserer Camp Adventure Academy in der Lüneburger Heide (Walsrode, Norddeutschland) an.

Camp Adventure ist auch Spezialist in Outdoor-Programmen und Aktivitäten, die von Abenteuerflair, Naturerlebnis, Teamgeist und Selbsterfahrung geprägt sind. Als Experte auf dem Gebiet Abenteuer- und Erlebnisfreizeit können wir auch Hotels, Resorts und Freizeitparks speziell im Bereich der Programm- und Anlagengestaltung optimale Beratung bieten.

Was wir bieten:

Internationale Sport- & Sprachcamps (Deutschland, England, Nordirland)

Unsere **Sport- & Sprachcamps** vereinen das internationale und ganz besondere Camp Adventure Feeling. Sprachunterricht, praktische Projekte mit Fokus auf dem Erlernen neuer Fähigkeiten und die Mischung aus Campspielen und Sportarten aller Art führen zu fantastischen Erlebnissen und Erfahrungen. Kommt und trefft viele neue Freunde in eurem Alter aus aller Welt in unseren internationalen Camps!

Erlebnispädagogische Klassenreisen (Deutschland)

Unsere kreativen und abenteuerlichen **Klassenreise Programme** zeichnen sich durch ihre Programmvielfalt und gut abgestimmte erlebnispädagogische Inhalte aus. Unser Ziel ist es die Klassengemeinschaft zu stärken und den Team Spirit zu wecken. Dies schaffen wir unter anderem durch eine individuelle Betreuung der Schülerinnen und Schüler. „Back to […] nature" lautet eins unserer Mottos. Bewusst entscheiden wir uns dafür, mal ein paar Tage „offline" zu sein und zu entspannen.

Camp Adventure Academy (Deutschland)

Als Spezialist in den Bereichen Erlebnispädagogik und Outdoor Sport, wurde die Academy bereits von vielen Schülerinnen und Schülern und Profis genutzt, um ihre Fähigkeiten im faszinierenden Bereich der Outdoor Education zu erweitern und / oder als Team zusammen zu wachsen. Seit 2015 hat sie ihr festes Zuhause in der Lüneburger Heide. Das Gelände ist durch seine Vielfältigkeit und Größe für eine Vielzahl von Aktivitäten und Veranstaltungen geeignet. Neben Klassenreisen und Jugendcamps bietet die Camp Adventure Academy auch die passende Location für Aus- und Fortbildungen, Firmenevents, Messen und Survival Kurse.

FAQs

Welche Sprachen werden im Camp gesprochen?

Die Hauptsprache in all unseren Camps ist zunächst Englisch. Dazu kommt die jeweilige Sprache des Landes, in dem das Camp stattfindet. Dadurch, dass wir unseren Hauptsitz in Deutschland haben, sind in allen Camps auch immer deutsche bzw. deutschsprachige Teamer dabei. Alle Ansagen und Erklärungen werden daher immer auf Deutsch und Englisch durchgeführt. Selbstverständlich stehen auch alle unsere Teamer mit ihren unterschiedlichen Nationalitäten für einzelne Übersetzungen zur Verfügung.

→ students' book, pages 130/131

Wie ist mein Kind im Camp untergebracht?

Im Adventure Camp Bayerischer Wald und in der Lüneburger Heide können die Juniors (7 – 12) und die Seniors (12 – 16) zwischen Zelt und Hütte wählen. Die Zelte sind mit einem Fußboden und einer Holz-Empore ausgestattet, pro Zelt werden 6 – 7 Personen untergebracht. Die Teilnehmerinnen und Teilnehmer können es sich mit Schlafsack und Isomatte gemütlich machen. Die Holzhütten sind mit Etagenbetten ausgestattet und bieten Platz für 4 – 8 Kinder. An den anderen Standorten werden die Teilnehmerinnen und Teilnehmer in Jugendherbergen, Sportzentren oder Internaten von Privatschulen in Mehrbettzimmern untergebracht. Ausführliche Informationen zur jeweiligen Unterbringung findet ihr auf den einzelnen Campseiten.

Gibt es verbotene Gegenstände?

Ja, die gibt es. Nicht erlaubt sind Taschenmesser, sämtliche Waffen, Feuerzeuge und Streichhölzer (Brandgefahr im Wald!). Drogen jeglicher Art, auch Alkohol und Zigaretten, gehören ebenfalls dazu.

www.campadventure.de

Sarah What is special about these camps?

You ____________________

____

____________________.

Sarah I love adventures! I can understand the word pocket knife in the last paragraph. Do we all have to take one?

You ____________________.

Sarah OK. Is there anything else that is not allowed?

You ____________________

____

____________________.

Sarah They often use the word 'camp'. Does that mean that we must go camping?

You ____________________

____________________.

Sarah As I'm in Germany at the moment, I'd like to spend the next holidays in an English-speaking region. Do these camps take place only in Germany?

You ____________________.

Sarah I can understand that they organize camps for classes. Can we only take part with our classmates?

You ____________________.

Sarah OK. Can you tell me why you think that these camps could be a good choice for us?

You ____________________

____

____________________.

My review

1 About my dream job

1 in
2 about
3 from
4 to
5 about / of
6 in
7 at
8 in
9 to
10 to

2 About part-time jobs

1 said
2 had applied
3 explained
4 was saving
5 mentioned
6 told
7 had
8 was
9 couldn't
10 not to worry
11 didn't start
12 would

3 About volunteering

1 The expert said there was a wide range of opportunities for young people.
2 She asked people to phone in with their questions.
3 She also told the listeners where they could find more information.
4 A teenage boy asked the expert how they selected volunteers.
5 A young girl wanted to know whether there was an age limit for volunteers.
6 Another caller asked if volunteers needed any special training.
7 A woman asked what would happen if she changed her mind.
8 The expert advised people not to apply if they weren't sure.

4 About children's rights

1 all
2 many
3 majority
4 a lot of
5 much
6 both
7 most
8 half
9 Most of
10 few

Appendix

Grammatical terms

adjective	Adjektiv
adverb **adverb of frequency** **adverb of manner** **adverb of place** **adverb of time**	Adverb Adverb der Häufigkeit Adverb der Art und Weise Adverb des Ortes Adverb der Zeit
adverbial	Adverbial
clause ***if*-clause** **main clause** **subordinate clause**	Teilsatz Konditionalsatz / Bedingungssatz Hauptsatz Nebensatz
comparative / superlative	Komparativ / Superlativ
conjunctions	Bindewörter
future **future with *going to*** **future with *will***	Futur Futur mit *going to* Futur mit *will*
gerund	Gerundium
infinitive	Infinitiv
negative / positive	negativ, verneint / positive, bejaht
noun	Nomen, Substantiv
subject / object	Subjekt / Objekt
past **simple past** **past progressive** **past perfect** **past perfect progressive**	Vergangenheit Imperfekt, Präteritum Verlaufsform des Präteritum Plusquamperfekt Verlaufsform der Vergangenheit
possessive determiner	Possessivbegleiter
present **simple present** **present progressive** **present perfect** **present perfect progressive**	Gegenwart Präsens Verlaufsform des Präsens Perfekt Verlaufsform des Perfekt
pronoun **possessive pronoun** **reciprocal pronoun** **reflexive pronoun**	Pronomen Possessivpronomen Reziprokpronomen Reflexivpronomen
quantifier	Zahlwort
question tag	Frageanhängsel
reported speech (indirect speech)	indirekte Rede
short answer	Kurzantwort
statement	Aussagesatz

Grammar

Do you have a question about grammar? The **grammar appendix** explains all the grammar that you learn in this book.

G 1 Gerund as subject

students' book, pages 14 – 15

A gerund is the *-ing* form of a verb. A gerund followed by an object or adverbial is called a gerund clause.

We can use a gerund or a gerund clause as the subject of a verb. This is when the subject is an activity or action.

Walking *can be dangerous here.*
Doing chores *isn't my favourite activity.*
Going to the shopping mall *is always fun.*

To form the negative, we put *not* before the gerund.
Not going out *on a Saturday evening is quite uncommon among teenagers in the USA.*

We often use the gerund as a subject in signs and notices.

See also → G2, G15, G16, G18, G28

G 2 Gerund as object

students' book, pages 14 – 15

A gerund is the *-ing* form of a verb. A gerund followed by an object or adverbial is called a gerund clause.

We can use a gerund or a gerund clause as the object of certain verbs. This is when the object is an activity or action.

I love ***cooking****.*
I don't mind ***sweeping the porch****.*
I like ***seeing how people live here****.*
He doesn't enjoy ***going to the gym****.*

To form the negative, we put *not* before the gerund.
I regret ***not going*** *to the school prom.*

See also → G1, G15, G16, G18, G28

G 3 Simple past and past progressive (revision)

students' book, pages 14 – 15

We use the simple past to talk about a completed action in the past.
*I **did** some chores this morning.*

We use the past progressive to talk about something in progress and unfinished at a specific time in the past.
*I **was doing** my chores at 10.00 this morning.*

We often use the simple past with the past progressive. This is when a shorter action happens at the same time as another action or 'interrupts' a longer action that is already in progress.
*Susan **called** round to see me while I **was doing** my chores.*

We often use ***when*** or ***while*** to link the actions. We use *when* before the simple past. We use *when* or *while* before the past progressive.

Examples

*I first **went** to America in 2010 when I **was studying** English at university.*
*I **saw** Ellie yesterday when we **were coming** home in the car.*
*My parents **were working** in New York when they first **met**.*
*Alex **phoned** me while we **were having** lunch yesterday.*

G 4 Relative pronouns (revision)

students' book, pages 18 – 19

We use relative pronouns in defining relative clauses to identify people and things. We use them in non-defining relative clauses to give extra information about someone or something.

The relative pronouns are ***who, which, that*** and ***whose***.
We use ***who*** for people and ***which*** for things.
In a defining relative clause, we can also use ***that*** for both people and things. We don't use *that* in a non-defining relative clause.

*Find out what life was like for the passengers **who / that** travelled aboard the Mayflower.*
*Relive the event **which / that** started the American Revolution!*
*Look! There are the people **who / that** we met yesterday.*
*The War of Independence, **which** led to the founding of the United States, took place in the 18th century.*

We use ***whose*** to show possession.
*Is that the man **whose** wallet you found?*
*You can also visit the homesite of the Wampanoag Indians, **whose** land this was.*

See also → G5, G6

G 5 Defining relative clauses (revision)

students' book, pages 18 – 19

A clause is a part of a sentence. A defining relative clause identifies a person, thing, place or time.

A defining relative clause comes immediately after this person, thing, place or time.

The relative clause begins with a relative pronoun (*who, which, that* or *whose*).

A descendant is related to a person ***who lived a long time ago****.*
Is this the museum ***that Alex recommended****?*
Step aboard a replica of the tiny ship ***which brought the Pilgrims to the New World****.*

A relative pronoun can be the subject or the object of a relative clause.

	RELATIVE PRONOUN / SUBJECT	VERB	OBJECT	
There's the man	*who*	*helped*	*us*	*yesterday.*

	RELATIVE PRONOUN / OBJECT	SUBJECT	VERB	
There's the man	*who*	*we*	*helped*	*yesterday.*

! We can leave out *who, which* or *that* when it is the object of the relative clause.

*There's the man (**who**) we helped yesterday.*
*The first community (**that**) the Pilgrims built when they arrived in 1620 was in Plymouth.*
*The book (**which**) you gave me is really interesting.*
*Is this the museum (**that**) Alex recommended?*

We don't leave out ***who***, ***which*** or ***that*** when it is the subject of the relative clause.
NOT ~~*There's the man helped us yesterday.*~~

See also → G4, G6

G 6 Non-defining relative clauses (revision)

students' book, pages 18 – 19

We use a non-defining relative clause to give extra, non-essential information about someone or something.

The relative clause begins with a relative pronoun (*who, which* or *whose*). Note that we don't use *that* in a non-defining relative clause.

We always separate a non-defining relative clause from the main clause with commas.

*George Washington, **who was born in 1732**, was the first president of the USA.*
*I live in Concord, **which is the capital of New Hampshire**.*
*A group of colonists, **whose leader was Samuel Adams**, boarded three British tea ships in Boston Harbor.*

We can also use a non-defining relative clause to comment on the whole of the previous clause.

*The British introduced many new taxes, **which the colonists thought was very unfair**.*
*The museum was closed, **which meant we had to go back the next day**.*

! Note that non-defining relative clauses are used mostly in writing and in other more formal contexts. Non-defining relative clauses that comment on a whole clause can be quite common in spoken English.

See also → G4, G5

G 7 The definite, indefinite and zero article

students' book, pages 24 – 25

As well as the basic rules regarding the use of the definite, indefinite and zero article, there are a number of special cases. These include:

We use ***the*** before:

- countries with a plural element (including words like States, Kingdom, Republic):
  *I'm from **the Netherlands**.* • *She's from **the USA**.* • *Have you been to **the United Kingdom**?*
- certain geographical regions and island groups:
  *He's from **the Midwest**.* • *I'd love to go to **the Far East**.* • *We went to **the Galapagos Islands**.*
- some famous buildings and man-made or natural landmarks:
  *We went up **the Empire State Building**.* • *I'd love to go to **the Grand Canyon**.*
- oceans, seas and rivers, and mountain ranges:
  *We swam in **the Pacific Ocean**.* • *Lake Itasca is the source of **the Mississippi**.* • *We flew over **the Rockies**.*
- groups of people or nations:
  ***The British** ruled America until 1776.* • ***The Chinese** invented fireworks.*

We use **no article** (zero article) before:

- continents, most countries, states or cities:
  *Have you ever been to **Asia**?* • *I used to live in **Turkey**.* • *She's from **New York**.*
- lakes and mountains:
  *I live near **Lake Ontario**.* • *We flew over **Mount Everest**.*
- languages:
  *I'm learning **English**.* • *Do you speak **German**?*

We use ***a / an*** before:

- jobs:
  *He's **a farmer**.* • *I want to be **an engineer**.* • *She's **a lawyer**.* • *Are you **a student**?*

G 8 Past perfect and simple past (revision)

students' book, pages 28 – 29

We use the past perfect to show that one event happened before another event in the past. We use the past perfect for the event that happened first and we use the simple past for the more recent event.

*A few hours after we **had started** along the trail, my father **fell** ill.*
*We **had hoped** to reach this place sooner, but the bad weather **slowed** us down.*

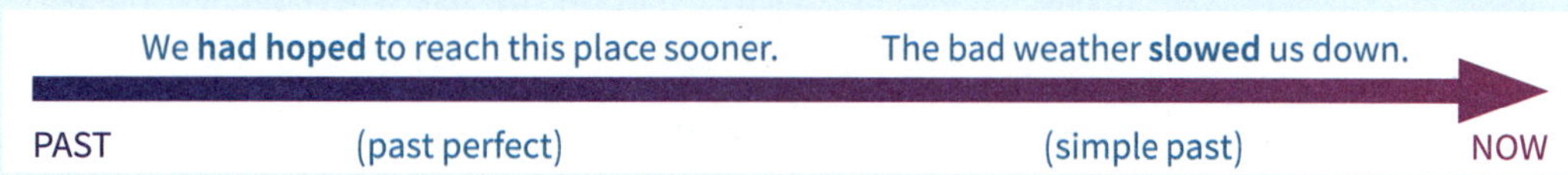

We also use the past perfect to show that something happened before a time in the past.
*We**'d travelled** over 200 miles **by 12 o'clock**.*

We often use sequence adverbs such as *when*, *before*, *after* and *until* to link the two events.
*The poor Parsons' boy **had** just **had** his 8th birthday **when** he fell and died.*

Examples
*We **went** for a walk after we**'d eaten** lunch.*
*The train **left** before I**'d got** on it.*
*I **had** never **slept** in a tent until last summer.*

See also → G9

G 9 Past perfect progressive

students' book, pages 28 – 29

We form the past perfect progressive with *had been* + verb + *-ing*.

*Settlers **had been camping** along the trail for many years before they came.*

We use the past perfect to show that one event happened before another event or before a specific time in the past.

We use the past perfect progressive to focus on the duration of the activity and / or to show that the activity was in progress or regularly repeated over a period of time.

*It **had been raining** a lot and the water was very high.*
*They**'d been travelling** for ten hours before they stopped to set up camp for the night.*

Examples

*We**'d been waiting** for over an hour before the bus arrived.*
*I was tired because I**'d been driving** all day.*
*She**'d been feeling** ill for a few days before she went to the doctor.*

See also → G 8

G 10 Present perfect (revision)

students' book, pages 46 – 47

We form the present perfect with *has / have* + past participle.

	Has / Have	Past participle	
I	***'ve***	***been***	*here for a few months.*
Morgan	***has***	***told***	*me about you.*
They	***haven't***	***arrived***	*yet.*

We form a question by putting the subject after the auxiliary verb *have*.

***Have they arrived** yet?*
*How long **have you lived** here?*

We use the present perfect in two main ways.

- To talk about something in the past which is connected with or has a consequence in the present. We often use the present perfect in this way with *yet* and *already*.

  *Mia, you haven't met Chris **yet**.*
  *I've **already** booked the tickets.*
  He's lost his keys.

- To talk about something that started in the past and continues now. We use the present perfect in this way with *for* and *since* with *all* and in questions with *How long*?

  *We've been friends **since** we were seven.*
  *He's known her **for** ten years.*
  *I've had problems with my computer **all** day. **How long** have you known Mia?*

See also → G 11, G 12

G 11 Present perfect progressive (revision)

students' book, pages 46 – 47

We form the present perfect progressive with *has / have been* + *-ing*.

	Has / Have been	*-ing*	
I	*'ve been*	*working*	*all day.*
It	*'s been*	*raining*	*since lunchtime.*
We	*haven't been*	*living*	*here for long.*

We form a question by putting the subject between *has / have* and *been*.
***Has he been** playing the drums for a long time?*
*How long **have you been** waiting?*

We use the present perfect progressive to talk about a continuous or repeated activity, or a situation that continues to the present.
*She**'s been listening** to jazz guitar all her life.*
*I**'ve been going** to a lot of concerts recently.*
*It**'s been raining** since I got up.*

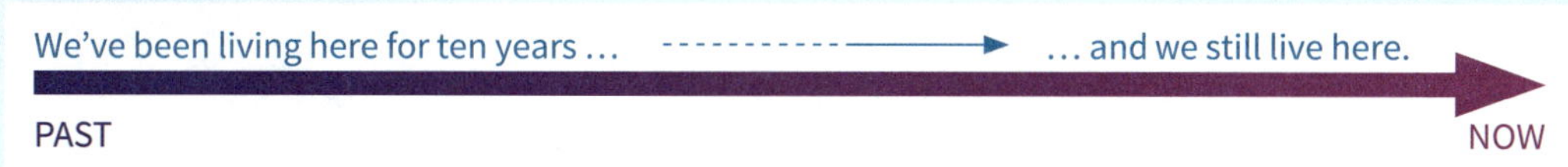

We use the present perfect in this way with *for* and *since* or with a time expression that connects the past with now (for example *recently*, *all her life*, *all afternoon*, *this week*, etc.).

! Remember that state verbs are generally not used in the progressive form.

*He**'s had** a trumpet since 2019.* NOT ~~*He's been having a trumpet since 2019.*~~
*We**'ve known** each other for ten years now.* NOT ~~*We've been knowing each other for ten years now.*~~

See also → G10, G12

G 12 Time words

students' book, pages 46 – 47

We can use *for*, *since*, *already*, *yet* and *ever* with the present perfect and the present perfect progressive.

- We use the present perfect + *for* or *since* when an action or situation started in the past and continues to the present.
- We use ***for*** + a period in time (e. g. *for ten minutes*, *for three days*, *for ages*, *for a long time*, etc.):
  *He's had that trumpet **for a long time**.*
  *We've been living here **for twenty years**.*
- We use ***since*** + a point in time (e. g. *since 3 o'clock*, *since July*, *since 2019*, *since my birthday*, etc.):
  *I've had this book **since I was a child**.* • *They've been practising **since 2 o'clock**.*
- We use ***already*** to talk about something that happened previously. *Already* usually goes between *have* and the main verb.
  *We've **already** seen that film.*
- We use ***yet*** to talk about something that hasn't happened, but is expected to happen. *Yet* usually goes at the end of the sentence.
  *I haven't seen the film **yet**.*
- We can use *Have you **ever** …?* to ask about life experiences.
  *Have you **ever** been to Japan?*

See also → G10, G11

G 13 *If*-sentences type 1 (revision)

students' book, pages 50 – 51

We use *if*-sentences type 1 to talk about things that are possible or likely to happen.
If-sentences type 1 have the form *if* + simple present, *will / won't* + infinitive.

*If I **think** something's cool, I'**ll go out** and buy it.*
*If the phone **is** too expensive, I **won't buy** it.*

We use *unless* to mean *if not*.
*We'll go for a walk **unless** it **rains**. = We'll go for a walk **if** it **doesn't rain**.*

We use *when* for things which will definitely happen.
***When** I get home, I'll call you.*

We can usually put the two clauses in any order. When the *if / when / unless* clause is first, there is a comma between the clauses.
If I like it, I'll buy it. *I'll buy it if I like it.*

Examples

*If we **miss** the bus, we'**ll walk** home.*
*If you **see** Jenny, **will** you **say** hello from me?*
*I'**ll call** you when I **get** to the city centre.*
*I'**ll buy** this shirt unless I **see** a nicer one.*

See also → G14, G25

G 14 *If*-sentences type 2 (revision)

students' book, pages 50 – 51

We use *if*-sentences type 2 to talk about things that are impossible, hypothetical or unlikely to happen.
If-sentences type 2 have the form *if* + simple past, *would / wouldn't* + infinitive.

*If I **had** more money, I'**d buy** a new phone.*
*If we **didn't buy** so much, it **would be** better for the environment.*
*If we **recycled** more, there **wouldn't be** so much waste.*

We often use *could* or *might* in an *if*-sentence type 2.
*If I had more money, I **could** buy a new phone.*

We can usually put the two clauses in any order. When the *if* clause is first, there is a comma between the clauses.
If I had more time, I'd read more books. *I'd read more books if I had more time.*

We can say *If I was* … or *If I were* … . However, we usually say *If I were you*, … .
*If I **was / were** richer, I'd travel round the world.*
*If I **were** you, I'd start saving!*

Examples

*If I **had** more time, I'**d help** you.*
*I'**d go out** this evening if I **didn't have** so much homework.*
*What **would** you **do** if you **found** a wallet in the street?*
*If I **had** a credit card, I'm sure I'**d spend** a lot more!*

See also → G13, G25

G 15 Verb + gerund or *to*-infinitive

students' book, pages 56 – 57

Sometimes we use two verbs together. The second verb adds information to what is expressed by the first verb. The second verb is usually the gerund (*-ing* form) or the *to*-infinitive.

We use the gerund after certain verbs. These include:
admit • avoid • can't stand • dislike • don't mind • enjoy • feel like • finish • give up • imagine • mention • miss • practise • recommend • suggest

*I **don't mind doing** chores in the house.*
*She **suggested having** some Italian food for dinner.*

We use the *to*-infinitive after certain verbs. These include:
agree • arrange • can afford • choose • decide • expect • hope • learn • manage • need • offer • plan • promise • refuse • seem • want • would like / love / hate / prefer

***I'm planning to do** a student exchange in the US next year.*
*I **want to study** languages at university.*

See also → G16, G17, G18, G19, G20, G28

G 16 Verbs followed by gerund or infinitive with no change of meaning

students' book, pages 56 – 57

Some verbs can usually be followed by either *-ing* or the *to*-infinitive with no or little difference in meaning. These include:
begin • continue • hate • like • love • prefer • start

*I **prefer doing** sport. – I **prefer to do** sport.*
*He **started learning** French when he was six. – He **started to learn** English when he was six.*

See also → G15, G17, G18, G19, G20, G28

G 17 Verb + object + *to*-infinitive

students' book, pages 56 – 57

Some verbs are followed by an object + *to*-infinitive. These include:
advise • allow • ask • choose • encourage • expect • help • invite • need • order • persuade • remind • tell • want • warn • would like

*My classmates **want me to join** the Math Club.*
*The teachers **allow us to call** them by their first names!*

When these verbs are in the passive, they are followed directly by the infinitive.
*We **are allowed to call** our teachers by their first names.*
*At school, I **was encouraged to study** languages.*

! Note that we can use some verbs (e. g. *ask, choose, expect, help, need, want*) with or without an object.

*We **expect to arrive** at 8.30.*	*We **expect them to arrive** at 8.30.*
*He **helped to tidy** the room.*	*He **helped us to tidy** the room.*

See also → G15, G16, G18, G19, G20

G 18 Verbs followed by gerund or infinitive with change of meaning

students' book, pages 56 – 57

Some verbs can be followed by the gerund or the *to*-infinitive but there is a difference in meaning. These verbs include:

Try
We use *try* + *-ing* when we do something to see what the results will be.
***Try going** to bed earlier so you aren't tired in the morning.*
*I **tried turning** the computer on and off, but the program still didn't work.*

We use *try* + *to*-infinitive when we attempt to achieve something.
*We **tried to move** the box, but it was too heavy.*
*I'm **trying to learn** the drums, so that I can join a band.*

Remember **and** ***forget***
We use *remember / forget* + *-ing* to talk about memories.
*Do you **remember going** to school for the first time?*
*I'll never **forget visiting** London. It was a great trip!*

We use *remember / forget* + *to*-infinitive to talk about doing / not doing something.
***Remember to phone** Alex.*
*Oh no! I **forgot to invite** Anna to the party.*

Stop
We use *stop* + *-ing* to talk about something ending or stopping.
*I **stopped studying** French last year.*
*I hope it **stops raining** soon.*

We use *stop* + *to*-infinitive to express the reason or purpose.
*Sorry I'm late. I **stopped to get** something to eat on the way.*
*I was working, but I **stopped to watch** TV for a while.*

See also → G15, G16, G17, G19, G20, G28

G 19 Infinitives after question words and *whether*

students' book, pages 60 – 61

We can use some verbs + question word + *to*-infinitive. These include:

ask • decide • discover • discuss • explain • find out • forget • know • learn • remember • talk about • understand • wonder

*Let's **talk about where to stay**.*
*I can't **decide who to invite** to the party.*

We can also use certain phrases + question word + *to*-infinitive.
***I'm not sure** where to go.*
***I have no idea** how to install the software.*
***Let me know** what to buy.*
***Do you know** how to get to the station?*

We can also use a *to*-infinitive after *whether*.
*We need to decide **whether to go** by train or by bus.*
*I'm not sure **whether to stay** here or go with them.*

See also → G15, G16, G17, G18, G20

G 20 Infinitives after superlatives and numbers

students' book, pages 60 – 61

We can use a *to*-infinitive after a phrase with a superlative adjective.

*The **easiest way to get** there is by bike.*
*Where's **the most interesting place to go?***
***The best time of year to visit** is September.*
*Who's **the oldest person to compete** in the Olympics?*

We can use a *to*-infinitive after a phrase with *last* or an ordinal number (*first, second, last,* etc.).

*Will **the last person to leave** please turn off the lights?*
*Chicago was **the first city to have** a Ferris wheel.*
*Who was **the second person to walk** on the moon?*

See also → G15, G16, G17, G18, G19

G 21 Question tags (revision)

students' book, pages 60 – 61

We form a question tag with an auxiliary verb (*do, have, be* or a modal verb) + pronoun (*you, he, she, it, they,* etc.). We use the same auxiliary verb as in the first part of the statement. For the simple present and simple past, we use a form of *do*.

We use a negative question tag after a positive statement.
*You **remember** when we rode on that big Ferris wheel, **don't** you?*
*Samantha **has** been to the UK, **hasn't** she?*

We use a positive question tag after a negative statement.
*The museum **wasn't** open, **was** it?*
*Richard **can't** speak German, **can** he?*

We use a question tag in two main ways:

- When we expect someone to agree with us. In this case, the intonation on the question tag falls.

  Chicago's great, isn't it? ↘

  You don't drink coffee, do you? ↘

- When we ask a real question, often to check something. In this case, the intonation on the question tag rises.

  She's from New York, isn't she? ↗

  They didn't go on the school trip, did they? ↗

Examples

*He's studying English, **isn't he**?*
*You like Indian food, **don't you**?*
*It didn't rain much, **did it**?*
*He has a holiday job, **doesn't he**?*
*Sara can play the guitar, **can't she**?*

G 22 Passive: present, past, *will*-future and modals

students' book, pages 78 – 79

We use the passive when we are more interested in what happens than in who does the action. This is usually because who does the action is obvious, unknown or not important.

We form the passive with a form of *to be* + past participle:

- present tense: *is / are* + past participle
- past tense: *was / were* + past participle
- present perfect: *has / have been* + past participle

Today, most goods ***are paid*** *for electronically.*
The first emails ***were sent in*** *the 1970s.*
Our lives today ***have been transformed*** *by technology.*
Will: We use *will be* + past participle.
Housework ***will be done*** *by home robots.*
Modal verbs: We use *can be / might be / may be,* etc. + past participle.
Our homes will be full of smart appliances that ***can be controlled*** *remotely.*
The new website ***might be launched*** *soon.*

! We sometimes use the passive with *by* when we want to say who or what does the action (the agent).
Today, many cashiers have been replaced ***by*** *self-service check-outs.*

Examples

The internet ***is used by*** *billions of people every day.*
The film ***was directed by*** *Christopher Nolan.*
A lot of progress ***has been made*** *in the field of medicine.*
Many jobs ***won't be done*** *by humans in the future.*
In the future, human tour guides ***may be replaced by*** *robots.*

See also → G 23, G 24

G 23 Passive: verbs with two objects

students' book, pages 82 – 83

Some active verbs have two objects: a direct and an indirect object.

SUBJECT	ACTIVE VERB	INDIRECT OBJECT	DIRECT OBJECT
His friend's dad	*offered*	*him*	*some of the wheels.*

In the passive, the indirect object becomes the subject.

SUBJECT	PASSIVE VERB	DIRECT OBJECT
He	*was offered*	*some of the wheels.*

There is also another less common active structure.

SUBJECT	ACTIVE VERB	DIRECT OBJECT	*TO*	INDIRECT OBJECT
His friend's dad	*offered*	*some of the wheels*	*to*	*him.*

In the passive, the direct object becomes the subject. This passive structure is less common.

SUBJECT	PASSIVE VERB	*TO*	INDIRECT OBJECT
Some of the wheels	*were offered*	*to*	*him.*

! Note that we can use both passive structures with *by* + agent.
He was offered some of the wheels by his friend's dad.
Some of the wheels were offered to him by his friend's dad.

Examples

We were taught English by Ms Evans.
First prize was awarded to David Jones.

See also → G 22, G 24

G 24 Passive infinitive

students' book, pages 82 – 83

The passive infinitive is formed with *to be* + past participle (e.g. *to be shown, to be met, to be invited*).

Some verbs (e.g. *arrange, ask, expect, hate, hope, like, need, plan, prefer, try, want, would like*) are followed by the *to*-infinitive. When there is passive meaning, these verbs are followed by the passive infinitive.

SUBJECT	VERB	PASSIVE INFINITIVE	
People	*don't need*	***to be shown***	*how it works.*
We	*hope*	***to be met***	*at the airport.*

Examples

*The company wanted the empty tins **to be returned**.*
*We have arranged for you **to be taken** to your hotel.*
*I expect **to be invited** to the ceremony.*
*The battery needs **to be charged** overnight.*

See also → G 22, G 23

G 25 *If*-sentences type 3 (revision)

students' book, pages 88 – 89

We use *if*-sentences type 3 to talk about something that didn't happen in the past. We talk about it in an imaginary or a hypothetical way.
If-sentences type 3 have the form *if* + past perfect, *would / wouldn't have* + past participle.

*If our talk **had been** more fun, more people **would have come**.*
*If you**'d got up** earlier, you **wouldn't have missed** the bus.*

We often use *'d* instead of *had* and *would*, especially in speaking and informal writing. We also often use *'ve* instead of *have*.
*If I**'d** known about the meeting, I**'d've** told you.*

We often use *could have* or *might* have in an *if*-sentence type 3.
*If I hadn't been ill last week, I **could have gone** to the meeting.*

We can usually put the two clauses in any order. When the *if* clause is first, there is a comma between the clauses.
If I had had more money, I would have bought it.
I would have bought it if I had had more money.

Examples

*If I**'d had** more time, I**'d have been able to** help you.*
*If we**'d left** earlier, we**'d have missed** the terrible traffic.*
*What **would** you **have done** if you **had been** in my situation?*
*If we **hadn't sat** next to each other on the bus, we **wouldn't have met** each other.*
*I**'d have gone out** last night if I **hadn't had** so much homework.*

See also → G 13, G 14

G 26 Conjunctions with future time clauses

students' book, pages 88 – 89

We often use conjunctions such as ***when***, ***while***, ***until***, ***before***, ***after***, ***as soon as*** and ***once*** to introduce an action that is going to happen in the future.

When we are talking about the future, we usually use the simple present after a time conjunction.

***When** I **think** of a way, I'll tell you.*
*I'll let you know **as soon as** I **arrive**.*

We can also use the present progressive after a time conjunction to express something in progress.
*Let's meet **the next time** you**'re visiting** Berlin.*

We can also use the present perfect after a time conjunction to emphasize that one action is completed before the other action.
***When** I**'ve finished** my presentation, I'll send it to you.*

When we begin with the time conjunction, we put a comma between the clauses.
When we get to the station, I'll call you.
I'll call you when we get to the station.

Examples

*Let's meet again before I **leave**.*
*I'll message you as soon as I **hear** any news.*
*I'll email you when I**'ve had** lunch.*
*As soon as we **get** the green light, we'll make a start.*

! We do not use a future form with *will* after the time conjunction.
~~*I'll call you as soon as I will arrive.*~~
~~*I'll email you when I will have had lunch.*~~

G 27 Future perfect

students' book, pages 92 – 93

We form the future perfect with ***will have*** + **past participle**.

SUBJECT	*will have*	PAST PARTICIPLE	
Space travel	*will have*	*become*	*a reality by 2050.*

We most commonly use the future perfect to talk about something completed at a point in the future.

*Humans **will have visited** Mars by 2050.*
*I'm sure we**'ll have arrived** by midnight.*

We can also use the future perfect for something not completed or something still in progress at a specific time in the future.

*I **won't have finished** the report by Friday.*
*We**'ll have lived** here for ten years next month.*

We often use the future perfect with *by*.
*We'll have finished the meeting **by** 10.30.*

G 28 Gerund after prepositions

students' book, pages 110 – 111

We use the gerund (*-ing* form) after a preposition or after a prepositional verb (verb + preposition).

*I've always dreamed **of becoming** an architect.*
*He's always been passionate **about cooking**.*
*We're thinking **of going** to the cinema tonight.*
*He apologized **for being** late.*
*My grandma thanked us **for helping** her.*

To form the negative, we put *not* before the gerund.
*She apologised **for not being** at the meeting.*

Useful prepositional verbs that are followed by a gerund include:

admit to • (dis)agree with • apologize for • be used to • benefit from • complain about • concentrate on • dream of • feel like • focus on • forget about • look forward to • result in • succeed in • talk about • think about • think of • use for • worry about

Examples

*We**'re used to seeing** our families regularly.*
*Annie **is looking forward to having** dinner with her friends on Saturday.*

See also → G2, G15, G16, G18

G 29 Statements in reported speech

students' book, pages 114 – 115

We can use *say* and *tell* to report what someone says. We use an indirect object after *tell*.
We do not use an indirect object after *add*, *describe*, *explain*, *mention* and *say*.

*He **told me** he was teacher.*	*He **said** he was a teacher.*
NOT ~~*He told he was a teacher.*~~	~~*He said me he was a teacher.*~~

We can use *that* when we are reporting. There is no rule about *that* and it is usually a personal choice.
*She **said that** she was hungry.* OR *She **said** she was hungry.*

When we report with a reporting verb in the past tense, we generally change the tense:

- present tense – *past tense*
  *I **work** in London – She told me she **worked** in London.*
- past tense / present perfect – past perfect
  *We **missed** the bus. – He admitted that they**'d missed** the bus.*
  *I**'ve** just **been** on holiday. – He mentioned he**'d** just **been** on holiday.*
- will – would
  *I**'ll** call you later. – She promised she**'d** call me later.*
- can – could
  *I **can't** fix it. – He explained he **couldn't** fix it.*
- must – had to
  *We **must** leave. – She said they **had to** leave.*

! We do not always change the tense. This is usually to show that something is still true or important.

*Jim **left** about ten minutes ago. – He said that Jim **left** about ten minutes ago.*
*I**'ll be** back in ten minutes. – She added she**'ll be** back in ten minutes.*

See also → G30

G 30 Questions, requests, advice and orders in reported speech

students' book, pages 120 – 121

Questions
We can report a question with *asked*. We can use an indirect object or no indirect object after *asked*.
Where do you work? – He ***asked me*** *where I worked.*
How much is it? – She ***asked*** *how much it was.*

For a *yes / no* question (without a question-word) we use *if or whether*.
Are you a student? – He asked me ***if*** *I was a student.*
Does Peter speak Spanish? – She wanted to know ***whether*** *Peter spoke Spanish.*

Requests
We can report a request with *asked* + indirect object + *to*-infinitive.
Could you help me? – Alex asked ***me to help*** *him.*
Can you wait for me, please? – She asked ***us to wait*** *for her.*

Orders and advice
We can report an order or advice with *told / advised* + indirect object + *(not) to*-infinitive.

Don't be late again. – He told ***me not to be*** *late again.*
You should apologize to them. – She advised ***me to apologize*** *to them.*

! Note that we generally, but not always, change the tense when we report questions with *asked*. → G 29

The word order is different from direct questions. The word order is the same as in a statement.
Where does he live? – She asked me where he lives.
When are we leaving? – He asked when we were leaving.
NOT ~~*She asked me where does he live.*~~ ~~*He asked when were we leaving.*~~

Examples
He asked me if I was OK.
She asked me where John lived.
Oliver asked me to phone him.
The receptionist asked us to wait a few minutes.
The teacher told the children to be quiet.
She told me to work harder.

See also → G 29

G 31 Quantifiers

students' book, pages 124 – 125

We use quantifiers to express the quantity of something. Quantifiers are words such as *all*, *most*, *some*, *a few*, *both*, *none*, *no*, *each*, *every*.

To talk about things / people in general, we use *all / most / many / some / a few / no* + plural noun or uncountable noun (without *the*).
***All children** have the right to an education.*
***Most countries** have free education.*
***Many people** don't have a job.*

We can also use *no* + singular noun.
*Today, **no child** should go hungry.*

To talk about things / people in a specific group, we use *all / most / many / some / a few / one / none* + *of* + *the / my / their* / etc. + plural noun or uncountable noun.
***All of my friends** were surprised.*
***All of my work** is interesting.*
***One of his ambitions** is to be a model.*
***None of the jobs** were interesting.*

We can also use *all / most / many / some / a few / one / none* + *of* + pronoun
***Most of them** have a summer job.*
***A few of us** are going to the meeting.*

We can also use *all* + *the / my / their / etc* + plural noun or uncountable noun (without *of*).
***All my friends** were surprised.*
*I spend **all my pocket money**.*

We use *each / every* + singular noun.
***Every child** has the right to express their opinion.*
*I need to speak to **each person**.*

To talk about two things, we use *both*. We use:
- *both* + plural noun
  *I like **both colours**.*
- *both (of)* + *the / my / these* / etc + plural noun
  ***Both of the jobs** were interesting.*
  ***Both my parents** speak English.*
- ***both of*** + pronoun
  ***Both of them** are teachers.*

We use a number of other expressions with *of* + plural or uncountable noun / pronoun, for example:
***The majority of** people here don't have a passport.*
***A large percentage of** them have never travelled abroad.*
***A lot of** people didn't vote in the election.*
***Three quarters of** the land is used for farming.*
***A third of** the population lives in poverty.*
***30 per cent of** 18-year-olds go to university.*
***Half of** the country is desert.*

We usually use these expressions without *the* to talk about things / people in general, but with *the* to talk about specific groups.
***Over 50 % of people** don't have a passport.*
***Over 50 % of the people** we interviewed don't have a passport.*

Irregular verbs

infinitive	simple past	present perfect	German
to **be**	**was / were**	**been**	sein
to **beat**	**beat**	**beaten**	schlagen
to **become**	**became**	**become**	werden
to **begin**	**began**	**begun**	beginnen, anfangen
to **blow**	**blew**	**blown**	blasen
to **break**	**broke**	**broken**	brechen
to **bring**	**brought**	**brought**	bringen
to **build**	**built**	**built**	bauen
to **burn**	**burned / burnt**	**burned / burnt**	(ver)brennen
to **buy**	**bought**	**bought**	kaufen
to **catch**	**caught**	**caught**	fangen
to **choose**	**chose**	**chosen**	auswählen
to **come**	**came**	**come**	kommen
to **cost**	**cost**	**cost**	kosten
to **cut**	**cut**	**cut**	schneiden
to **deal**	**dealt**	**dealt**	handeln
to **do**	**did**	**done**	tun
to **draw**	**drew**	**drawn**	zeichnen
to **dream**	**dreamed / dreamt**	**dreamed / dreamt**	träumen
to **drink**	**drank**	**drunk**	trinken
to **drive**	**drove**	**driven**	fahren
to **eat**	**ate**	**eaten**	essen
to **fall**	**fell**	**fallen**	fallen, stürzen
to **feed**	**fed**	**fed**	füttern
to **feel**	**felt**	**felt**	(sich) fühlen, spüren
to **fight**	**fought**	**fought**	kämpfen
to **find**	**found**	**found**	finden

infinitive	simple past	present perfect	German
to **fly**	**flew**	**flown**	fliegen
to **forget**	**forgot**	**forgotten**	vergessen
to **forgive**	**forgave**	**forgiven**	vergeben
to **get**	**got**	**got / gotten**	bekommen, holen
to **give**	**gave**	**given**	geben, schenken
to **go**	**went**	**gone**	gehen, fahren
to **grow**	**grew**	**grown**	wachsen, anbauen
to **have (got)**	**had**	**had**	haben
to **hang**	**hung**	**hung**	hängen
to **hear** [ɪə]	**heard** [ɜː]	**heard** [ɜː]	hören
to **hide** [haɪd]	**hid** [hɪd]	**hidden**[hɪdn]	sich verstecken; etw. verstecken
to **hit**	**hit**	**hit**	schlagen
to **hold**	**held**	**held**	halten
to **hurt**	**hurt**	**hurt**	wehtun
to **keep**	**kept**	**kept**	(be)halten
to **kneel**	**knelt**	**knelt**	knien
to **know**	**knew**	**known**	wissen, kennen
to **lay**	**laid**	**laid**	legen
to **learn**	**learned / learnt**	**learned / learnt**	lernen
to **lead**	**led**	**led**	führen, leiten
to **leave**	**left**	**left**	verlassen
to **lend**	**lent**	**lent**	leihen
to **let**	**let**	**let**	lassen
to **lie**	**lay**	**lain**	liegen

infinitive	simple past	present perfect	German
to **light**	**lit / lighted**	**lit / lighted**	anzünden, anmachen
to **lose**	**lost**	**lost**	verlieren
to **make**	**made**	**made**	machen, herstellen
to **mean** [iː]	**meant** [e]	**meant** [e]	bedeuten
to **meet**	**met**	**met**	(sich) treffen, kennenlernen
to **pay**	**paid**	**paid**	bezahlen
to **put**	**put**	**put**	stellen
to **quit**	**quit**	**quit**	kündigen; verlassen
to **read** [iː]	**read** [e]	**read** [e]	lesen
to **ride**	**rode**	**ridden**	reiten, (Fahrrad) fahren
to **ring**	**rang**	**rung**	klingeln
to **rise**	**rose**	**risen**	wachsen, aufgehen
to **run**	**ran**	**run**	laufen, rennen
to **say** [eɪ]	**said** [e]	**said** [e]	sagen
to **see**	**saw**	**seen**	sehen
to **sell**	**sold**	**sold**	verkaufen
to **send**	**sent**	**sent**	schicken
to **set**	**set**	**set**	setzen, stellen, legen
to **shake**	**shook**	**shaken**	schütteln
to **shine**	**shone**	**shone**	scheinen
to **shoot**	**shot**	**shot**	schießen
to **show**	**showed**	**shown / showed**	zeigen
to **sing**	**sang**	**sung**	singen

infinitive	simple past	present perfect	German
to **sit**	**sat**	**sat**	sitzen
to **sleep**	**slept**	**slept**	schlafen
to **smell**	**smelled / smelt**	**smelled / smelt**	riechen
to **speak**	**spoke**	**spoken**	sprechen
to **spend**	**spent**	**spent**	verbringen, (Geld) ausgeben
to **spit**	**spat / spit**	**spat / spit**	spucken
to **spoil**	**spoilt**	**spoilt**	verderben
to **stand**	**stood**	**stood**	stehen
to **steal**	**stole**	**stolen**	stehlen
to **stick**	**stuck**	**stuck**	kleben
to **sting**	**stung**	**stung**	stechen
to **strike**	**struck**	**struck**	zuschlagen; streiken
to **swear**	**swore**	**sworn**	schwören
to **sweep**	**swept**	**swept**	fegen
to **swim**	**swam**	**swum**	schwimmen
to **take**	**took**	**taken**	nehmen, dauern
to **teach**	**taught**	**taught**	unterrichten
to **tell**	**told**	**told**	erzählen
to **think**	**thought**	**thought**	denken
to **throw**	**threw**	**thrown**	werfen
to **understand**	**understood**	**understood**	verstehen
to **wake**	**woke**	**woken**	erwachen; wecken
to **wear**	**wore**	**worn**	tragen
to **win**	**won** [ʌ]	**won**	gewinnen
to **write**	**wrote**	**written**	schreiben

Acknowledgements

Text credits

S. 30/31: „Open-Air Museum Hagen", LWL-Freilichtmuseum Hagen, https://www.lwl-freilichtmuseum-hagen.de/de/; S. 55: „What we do", Brooklyn Free School, https://www.brooklynfreeschool.org/; S. 80: „Erfindungen von Kindern", Deutsches Kinderhilfswerk e. V., 28. Mai 2018, https://www.kindersache.de/bereiche/wissen/natur- und-mensch/erfindungen-von-kindern; S. 105/106: „Camp Adventure", Camp Adventure e. K., https://www.campadventure.de/de/

Picture credits

|akg-images GmbH, Berlin: 7.3. |Alamy Stock Photo, Abingdon/Oxfordshire: Aerial Archives 53.1; Alpha Historica 66.1; Berger, Ira 42.2; Bildagentur-online/Ohde 85.1; Boethling, Joerg 103.1; Burlakov, Dmitry 97.3; Caddick, Bob 46.2; Cavan Images 97.2; chombosan 61.1; CHROMORANGE / Czerski, Titus E. 19.1; Clynt Garnham Education 48.1; Cultura Creative RF 40.2; Daniel Dempster Photography 33.1; dmac 46.1; eye35 52.1; Geopix 78.2; Grubka , Michael 42.1; Horree, Peter 36.1; Huseynaliyev, Dashqin 86.1; incamerastock 49.1; Incite Photography 22.1; Jannsen, Brian 50.1; Johnsson, Inge 23.2; KURKIN NIKOLAY 63.1; Lund, Jacob 40.1; Lupson, James 96.1; Machado, Nando 76.1; PhotoAlto 88.1; Prostock-studio 98.1; public domain sourced / access rights from Geopix 74.1; Rozalsk, Rafal 50.2; Sackermann, Joern 30.1; Segre, Alex 20.1; Smetzer, Don 104.1; Sriskandan, Kumar 23.1; Wavebreakmedia Ltd UC64_65 64.1; Zoonar GmbH 30.2. |Alamy Stock Photo (RMB), Abingdon/Oxfordshire: Aun, Kairi 99.1; Barnes, Stephen/Business 100.1; Cribb, Andrew 12.1; Croke, Tom 16.1; Dakowicz, Maciej 97.1; david pearson 72.1; Dinodia Photos 101.1; Duchaine, Randy 15.1; GREG RYAN 24.3; May, Steven 60.1; public domain sourced / access rights from NASA Image Collection 78.1; Smetzer, Don 24.2; Sriskandan, Kumar 91.1; Wheatley, Michael 43.1; World History Archive 59.1. |Domke, Franz-Josef, Hannover: 35.1, 54.1. |Donnelly, Karen, Brighton: 10.1, 11.1, 11.2, 11.3, 69.1, 81.1, 110.1, 110.2. |fotolia.com, New York: macrovector 94.3. |iStockphoto.com, Calgary: Branimir76 110.3; DenisTangneyJr 93.1; Highwaystarz-Photography 58.1; izusek 111.1; jenifoto 80.1; Newman Studio 70.1; Photoservice 21.1; rabbit75_ist 13.1; Roi and Roi 94.4; seb_ra 114.1; sodafish 37.1; sturti 67.1; TopVectors 94.1; TriggerPhoto 24.1; UnitoneVector 94.2. |Shutterstock.com, New York: Allard One 119.1; Anton_Ivanov 7.2; Besen, Heidi 7.1; chrisdorney 17.1; cowardlion 29.1; Everett Historical 18.1; Fields, Lara 6.1; Foltin, Anton 26.1; Guillem, Antonio 121.1; Habich, Arina P 116.1; ImageFlow 45.1; kavram 25.1; Mercado, Christina Yvonne 58.2; Motortion Films 124.1; Prostock-studio 38.1, 55.1; Supannee_Hickman 14.1; Valmedia 71.1; Venomous Vector 67.2. |Wildfang GbR Video & Audio Produktion, Berlin: 92.1.

Wir arbeiten sehr sorgfältig daran, für alle verwendeten Abbildungen die Rechteinhaberinnen und Rechteinhaber zu ermitteln. Sollte uns dies im Einzelfall nicht vollständig gelungen sein, werden berechtigte Ansprüche selbstverständlich im Rahmen der üblichen Vereinbarungen abgegolten.

Audio credits

Recorded at Dsound, London; recording engineer Mark Smith; produced by Anne Rosenfeld for RBA Productions